BAMBOOS

BAMBOOS

Photographs PAUL STAROSTA
Text YVES CROUZET

EVERGREEN

The world

of bamboo

*E*very day, bamboo is used in one form or another, at home or in the workplace, by over half the world's population. Its many and varied uses – from house-building to cookery, from hunting to making music, from transport to medicine, from a source of food to a source of inspiration – give some idea of just how greatly undervalued this plant is in the West.

This book considers various aspects of bamboo, including its symbolic, artistic, and cultural importance, and above all its ornamental value.

The photography has deliberately focused on the sort of details that go unnoticed by the casual observer, in order to highlight all the different features of bamboos and their truly magical qualities.

Botanically speaking, bamboos belong to the Gramineae (formerly Poaceae) family, which includes the grasses used in domestic lawns, and cereals such as wheat, maize, and oats. They are found in the wild in Asia, Africa, Australia, and America, between 40°N and 40°S. The bamboos that grow in Europe, on the other hand, are not indigenous and have all been introduced since the eighteenth century.

The main stem of the Gramineae is known as the culm* and, in the case of bamboos, it is from this culm (or cane) that the leaf-bearing branches emerge. (The culm of the larger bamboos is often referred to incorrectly as the "trunk".) Some species of bamboo, known as herbaceous bamboos, do not have rigid stems and are rarely cultivated, for either practical or ornamental purposes. The woody bamboos, on the other hand, whose culms are hard and resilient, are widely cultivated. This book focuses on the woody species, or at least on some of them, since there are over a thousand different species worldwide divided into almost seventy genera* (groups). This does not, of course, include any of the variants yet to be discovered in relatively unexplored regions of the world.

Since Carl von Linné (1707–1778) established the binomial system of biological nomenclature, plants have been classified on the basis of their flowers. The fact that bamboos rarely flower makes the botanist's task more difficult, which is why the nomenclature of the Gramineae is constantly changing. The names used here are those most commonly found in books and articles on bamboos, even though they may not always be strictly – that is, botanically – correct.

Anatomy

A bamboo consists of five basic parts: the rhizomes, the roots, the culms (canes), the branches, and the leaves. In addition, it may also bear flowers or fruit, sometimes both at the same time.

The **rhizomes*** are underground stems which are divided into sections by regularly spaced nodes. The buds that form on these nodes can develop into either new rhizomes or culms. As will be seen later, the type of rhizome – whether it is clumping (pachymorphic*) or running* (leptomorphic*), whether it grows monopodially* or sympodially* – determines the habit and general appearance of the bamboo.

The **roots** are branched to a greater or lesser degree, and are relatively slender (with a diameter of only a fraction of an inch). There are two types of roots. The first, which supply the plant with nutrients and water absorbed from the soil, occur along the length of the rhizomes, around the nodes. Roots of the second type develop at the base of the culm. Their main purpose is to ensure that the culm is firmly anchored in the soil and to prevent the plant falling over under the weight of its leaves or being blown over by the wind. These roots develop as soon as the young shoot* emerges from the soil.

Left

Semiarundinaria fastuosa

The **culms** (or canes) develop from underground rhizome buds and grow upwards. Like rhizomes, culms are divided into sections by regularly spaced nodes. These sections, known as internodes*, are generally hollow. The few varieties with solid internodes are known as "male" bamboos (although this should not be taken to imply that the plant has a "sex"). The buds around the nodes develop into leaf-bearing branches.

The **branches** emerge from the nodes of the culm, and then divide and branch before finally bearing leaves. The number of branches emerging from a node can be a useful indication of the genus (or group to which the bamboo belongs). For example, members of the genus *Phyllostachys* always have two branches per node. The branches have the same segmented structure as the culms and rhizomes.

The **leaves** borne by the branches produce the chlorophyll essential for photosynthesis. Bamboos also have another special type of leaf known as the ocrea* (or culm sheath), whose main function is to protect the young shoots. These

sheaths provide protection even before the shoots emerge from the soil, since they form as soon as the bud swells. There is one sheath for each internode. When the internode has finished growing, its texture changes within the space of a few days: the relatively soft consistency of the growing shoot is replaced by the shell-like casing of the culm (this does not apply to herbaceous bamboos). The sheath is now of no further use and, in most species, dries up and is discarded by the plant. In certain species, however, the sheath dries up but remains attached to the culm. These culm sheaths are extremely useful for classifying bamboos since their form, colour, and texture vary according to the species. The rhizomes are also protected by a similar type of sheath.

The **flowers.** Bamboos very rarely flower. A single species can go for dozens of years, and sometimes for over a century, without flowering. When flowering does finally occur, it can be universal, which means that it takes place simultaneously throughout the world for all the plants of the same clone* or generation. These gregarious* flowerings are

Above

Phyllostachys pubescens
(young roots)

often extremely prolific, with a single plant covered in thousands of flowers. Ironically, this profusion can sometimes prove fatal. The root stock, drawing on its reserves to support the growth of so many flowers, may never recover. However, the flowers are usually followed by the **fruit** and seeds and, even though the plant may have been exhausted by the flowering process, one seed is technically enough to ensure the perpetuation of the species. Even so, it would appear that some species of bamboo have died out altogether.

The seeds of bamboo, like those of wheat, are caryopses* and can be used to produce a flour that makes delicious bread. However, production on a regular basis would be impossible, since the seed supply depends upon the rather unpredictable life-cycle of the bamboo. This unpredictability more than justifies the role of conservatories, botanical gardens, and collections, where bamboos can be planted, catalogued, and closely monitored, and where fruits and seeds can be produced under controlled conditions. The process is a prime example of nature being given a helping hand by human beings, in this instance by removing the ripe caryopses from the plant and sowing them in light, sandy soil which is kept moist and warm. In a few days, the seeds germinate and produce a new generation of bamboo that will not flower for another, or possibly even two or three, human generations.

No-one has ever been able to explain why a specific group of bamboos should flower simultaneously throughout the world. It is not enough to say that these plants have been "genetically programmed" to flower at the same time, and researchers in a number of countries are currently working on this question. Three Indian scientists (Nadgauda, Parasharami, and Mascarenhas) recently brought a bamboo into flower under laboratory conditions at the Dera Dun research centre. Their breakthrough means that we can envisage controlling the flowering and fruiting process of bamboos within the foreseeable future. In other words, it will soon be possible to encourage bamboos to flower or, alternatively, to prevent a process that is potentially fatal for the plant. From here, it is not hard to imagine entire fields of bamboo producing an annual crop of caryopses or "grain". The fact that these fields would not have to be replanted every year would have definite advantages for regions where planting schedules are often disrupted by monsoons, hurricanes, or simply by heavy rain. Bamboo could well be the cereal crop of the third millennium, although this would only be part of the role it would be required to play. Controlled flowering would also make it possible to produce hybrids in which certain characteristics are enhanced and others suppressed. In other words, "customized" varieties of bamboo could be produced to suit a wide range of different climates and requirements: for instance bamboo shoots to accompany the Sunday roast, bamboo for construction purposes or to meet the ever-increasing demands of the world's paper mills, and, last but by no means least, a bamboo supply to reduce the demands on the world's natural resources which, if they continue at the present rate, will ultimately endanger the ecological balance of the whole planet. Bamboo could well be the solution to a number of global problems. Even on a relatively modest scale, it almost certainly has an important role to play in the future relationship between mankind and the biosphere, and the inevitable reassessment of human attitudes towards Nature.

The physiology of bamboo

Bamboo culms have achieved their ultimate diameter by the time they emerge from the soil. It then takes them between 2 and 4 months to reach their final height. Surprisingly, temperate bamboos grow faster than tropical species. In western Europe, for example, the culms of *Phyllostachys pubescens* have a diameter of 18–22 cm (7–8½ in) as they emerge from the ground. Eight weeks later, they have reached a height of over 20 m (64 ft). The nodes of the culms are already formed when the young shoots or turions* emerge from the ground, but are concertinaed together. They open out like a telescope as the internodes gradually extend, growing as much as 1 m (3 ft) in 24 hours! Bamboos are in fact the fastest growing plants in the entire vegetable kingdom, a phenomenon that is explained by their physiology.

The energy absorbed by the leaves during photosynthesis is stored in the rhizomes and used later by the turions. The growth of the turions is very different from the growth of seeds, whose reserves are used to produce the first roots and leaves. The seedling then takes over, absorbing the nutrients (via its roots) and the energy (via its leaves) that it requires in order to continue growing. This process is impossible for the turion since the leaves do not develop until it has reached its ultimate diameter and height and become an "adult" culm. Once it is fully grown, the culm produces the reserves required for the following year's shoots. This activity is intense during the first few years of the culm's life and then gradually slows down until the culm becomes inactive. It remains in leaf for several more years, although it makes no further contribution to the development of the group. The term "group" is particularly apt since a bamboo is not an individual plant, but a collection of culms, each with its own particular role. The young culms are fed and protected by the "adult" culms, which are the active members of the group. These "adult" culms were themselves fed and protected by the older culms that have since become inactive and will soon die, but without affecting the overall balance of the group.

The turions' growing season depends on the species of bamboo: spring or early summer for temperate bamboos, and late summer or autumn for tropical varieties. When the culms have finished growing, it is the turn of the rhizomes. There is often a rest period or rather a period of reduced activity in response to cold or drought.

A plant with a cultural history

To say that bamboo has a cultural history is not over-stating the case for a plant that, over centuries, has played a vital role in the lives of billions of people throughout the world. Although bamboo is usually associated with Asia, its role in Central and South America should not be under-estimated. It may not have been "venerated" to quite the same degree, but it has been used for practical purposes in these countries since the time of the Incas.

To avoid over-diversifying, this section concentrates on the cultural history of bamboo in Asia, and especially in China and Japan.

Bamboo not only forms an integral part of Chinese tradition and culture, but has also provided the tools and medium for transmitting that culture. The calligrapher's brush and writing tablets were both made of bamboo, and the first books were made from fine bamboo tablets artistically bound together. At the beginning of the second century AD, the first paper was made from bamboo fibres. Fine layers of bamboo pulp, obtained by soaking and kneading the fibres, were dried on racks that were also made of bamboo. When dry, the layers were pressed to obtain sheets of paper. Today, China's huge modern paper mills transform bamboo into paper, although small craft workshops are still using the ancient methods, which have remained virtually unchanged.

Calligraphers' brushes are nearly always made of bamboo, at least the handle is bamboo and the bristles are made of animal hair. In the past, the early Buddhists' respect for all living creatures made them reluctant even to pluck the hairs from their bodies. Once again, bamboo provided the solution. Unlike the crosswise structure of other woody plants, the length-wise, parallel structure of bamboo fibres meant that those at the end of a piece of bamboo could be easily separated, and the entire brush – handle and 'bristles' – could be made from a single piece of bamboo.

As well as playing a major role in the art of calligraphy, bamboo is also a leitmotif in Chinese paintings. Indeed, in *The Book of Bamboo,* David Farrelly compares the role of bamboo in Oriental art to that of the nude in Western art and sculpture.

Bamboo is often used to symbolize the Daoist principle of giving way before external pressures in order to transcend them. The image of bamboo, bending beneath the force of the wind but regaining its former stature and splendour when the storm is over, is particularly apt. Bamboo also has great symbolic value for Buddhists, who refer to it as a "blessing from heaven". According to the teachings of Gautama Siddhartha, better known as the Buddha (?563–483 BC), bamboo enables the individual to achieve a state of inner peace. He in fact prepared for his own death by withdrawing to a forest of bamboo.

The great Chinese poet Su Dongpo (or Su Shi, 1036–1101 AD) lived during the Song dynasty (960–1279 AD), a period renowned for its art, literature and philosophy. He was also an artist, writer and philosopher, and wrote of bamboo: "It is possible to prepare a meal without meat, but not to build a house without bamboo. Without meat, we lose weight, but without bamboo we lose our identity, the very essence of our culture."

Bamboo also features prominently in Japanese art and culture. From the fifteenth century, it was used to make the utensils for the Japanese tea ceremony, for example the brush split into 120 curved strips used to mix the tea. The ritual of the tea ceremony reflects the desire of the participants to achieve a state of inner peace and balance in harmony with the elements, a dimension sadly absent from Western society.

An entire book would not suffice to describe the role of bamboo in the art and traditions of Japan. Its essence can perhaps best be expressed by Japanese haiku, a verse form influenced by Zen Buddhism. These short poems are extremely simple but highly evocative, and seem to emanate from the reader rather than the writer.

Toad
Be so kind as to move to one side
And let me plant these bamboos
(Chora)

Bright droplets in the morning!
Sound of the dew
Dripping in the bamboo
(Buson)

A gust of winter wind
Rushing through the bamboo
And suddenly calm
(Basho)

The symbolism of bamboo

In China, bamboo symbolizes humility and modesty, as well as eternal youth – probably because of its evergreen foliage and longevity – and alertness in old-age. The culms look the same whether they are a few months or a few years old. It also symbolizes joy and laughter, peace and serenity, good fortune and happiness, flexibility, steadfastness, and persistence. In Vietnam, bamboo is considered to be "the brother of Man". In Japan, it is one of the "three friends" – bamboo, blossoming plum, and pine – that form the basis of traditional New Year decorations. The plum and bamboo are also two of the "four noble plants" that symbolize happiness for the Chinese, the other two being the orchid and the chrysanthemum.

Bamboo is used in religious ceremonies, especially Indonesian cremations. Some species, *Schizostachyum brachycladum* for example, are particularly sought after for this purpose. In the past, the Chinese used bamboo as a sort of firecracker. They threw it into the fire in the belief that the noise of the exploding internodes would drive away evil spirits and enable the gods to grant wishes and prayers. According to one theory, the Malaysians derived the word "bamboo" from the cracking noise (*bam!*) made as the stem exploded under the pressure created by hot air trapped between the nodes, and the sound (*boooo…*) of the escaping air.

Bamboo can also inspire a code of conduct: "Make sure your life is as pure and straight as a bamboo flute" (R. Tagore), or describe a particular bent of character. In Japan, for example, it is applied to someone who is flexible and prepared to adapt to changing situations, who knows when to give way in order to emerge unscathed and with dignity from difficult situations. The Chinese also compare themselves to bamboo, bending beneath the weight of their destiny but

remaining unbroken by misfortune. Although bamboo is not, historically speaking, part of Western culture, the opportunity is certainly there for the future. According to Thomas Jefferson, "the greatest service done to any culture is the introduction of a new agricultural crop", and there is no doubt that bamboo has a great deal to offer the West in the fields of agriculture and gardening. After all, the tomato and the potato, both introduced from South America, now form an integral part of Western cuisine.

Left

Pleioblastus hindsii

Bamboos in the garden

In the West, bamboos are divided into four groups. The classification, which is horticultural rather than botanical, is purely practical and is based on the ultimate height of the bamboos. However, it is not infallible and should be treated with caution since growth is dependent on a plant's environment, and a bamboo that struggles to reach 5–6 m (16–20 ft) under one set of conditions will easily grow to a height of 20 m (64 ft) in a different situation. The heights given below are those achieved under favourable conditions. Bamboos are classified as "dwarf" under 1.5 m (5 ft), "small" between 1.5 and 3 m (5–10 ft), "medium-sized" between 3 and 9 m (10–29 ft), and "tall" over 9 m (29 ft).

When choosing a bamboo, it is essential to take account of local conditions. Climate can be a determining – and limiting – factor. It should be remembered that the growth of the culms is dependent on the reserves stored by the plant during the previous year. These reserves are created by photosynthesis and are therefore determined by the amount of sunlight to which the plant is exposed. Medium-sized and tall bamboos will therefore do less well in more northerly regions. The height of bamboos is also adversely affected by poorly aerated and poor-quality soil.

Above

Phyllostachys fimbriligula

Climate

There are two categories of bamboo classified according to climate: tropical bamboos and temperate bamboos.

Apart from a few extremely well-protected regions where winters are very mild, tropical bamboos cannot be grown out of doors in Europe. Even in these milder regions, it is important to choose the hardier species. *Bambusa multiplex* and its cultivars* are among the most frost-resistant tropical bamboos. Provided the frosts are not too early (the young shoots develop in autumn), they will withstand temperatures of up to -9°C (16°F).

Frost can affect bamboos at three different levels:

– At the first level the leaves are affected. If the leaf cells cannot withstand the frost, they burst, and the leaves dry out. Provided the frost is relatively light, the buds in the axil of each leaf will not be affected and will produce new leaves in the spring. At worst, the bamboo will look rather sad for a few weeks.

– If the frost is harder and lasts longer, it will destroy the buds as well as the leaves. The damage can be assessed after a few days, using a strong magnifying glass as the buds are still very small. Only the buds that survive will produce leaves. But even if all the buds have been frosted, the bamboo still has its underground reserves.

– If all the buds are frosted, it is advisable to cut back the damaged culms as they will be replaced by the following spring's new growth. However, it is important to take certain precautions as the root stock will react by producing turions earlier than it would under normal circumstances. If these turions emerge too soon, they will also run the risk of being frosted since the thick foliage of the old culms is not there to protect them. The best way to stop the turions emerging is to prevent the soil warming up too soon, and this can be done by covering the plant with a thin layer of straw, wood shavings, or peat. However, if the layer is too thick, the temperature can rise to over 60°C (140°F), even in the depths of winter. Not only will this trigger the growth of the buds, but the heat generated by the layer will "cook" them as they pass through it.

Bamboo, soil, and water

Bamboos dislike too little or too much water. They do not grow well in waterlogged soil and only *Arundinaria gigantea* and possibly *Phyllostachys heteroclada* will survive in such conditions. In the case of all other bamboos, the rhizomes must be able to breathe.

Well-established bamboos can generally survive drought by "shutting down" and conserving moisture by curling their leaves around the central vein. Although they look more like skeletal conifers than lush plants, they can survive for weeks and even months in this way, provided the roots can draw just enough moisture from the subsoil to keep them "ticking over". As soon as they receive sufficient quantities of water, it takes less than an hour for the leaves to uncurl and for the plant to recover its graceful and elegant appearance, but this does not mean it has not suffered. The effects will inevitably be felt the following year since, during this critical period, the plant was unable to store up the reserves needed to feed the next season's new shoots. Whereas a well-established bamboo – even though it will not be the happiest of plants – can survive for long periods without water, recently planted and container-grown bamboos are an entirely different matter. Their relatively small root system means that the roots cannot absorb enough moisture for them to survive more than a few days. It is therefore essential to keep them well watered during long periods of dry weather or drought.

The ideal soil for most bamboos is light and friable, water retentive but well drained, and rich in nutrients and organic matter. However, although the quality of the soil is important it is not paramount. Bamboos also do well in ordinary garden soil, and even poor soils sometimes produce some very good results. Rather than trying to achieve the ideal soil type, it is far more important to ensure that plants are not subjected to harmful conditions that could prove fatal. The first of these is over-watering, although this does not immediately spring to mind when looking at the superb pictures of bamboos on the banks of China's Mekong River. However, a closer look reveals that these huge

Gramineae are always planted above the water line, so that even though their roots are occasionally submerged by floodwater, this lasts only a matter of hours or days.

Bamboos should not be planted in an area liable to flooding or places likely to be waterlogged for more than a week. The plants are not in fact killed by the water, but suffocate for lack of air. It is possible to prevent water collecting around the roots by creating a drainage system, increasing the angle of a slope or by planting on ridges. In this respect, the choice of site is extremely important.

Like many other plants, bamboos do not like salty soil, although *Phyllostachys iridescens* and *Phyllostachys fimbriligula* have a higher level of tolerance. Bamboos are in fact far less tolerant of chlorine than they are of salt, so chlorine-based fertilizers and watering regularly with water from the swimming pool are definitely not to be recommended.

Although bamboos will tolerate a certain level of calcium, they do not like excessive amounts and much prefer neutral or acid soils. Some varieties, *Phyllostachys flexuosa* for example, are more suited to earth with a high pH level. If planted in chalky soil, an intense yellowing of the leaves can be a sign of chlorosis*. However, an application of iron chelate* will restore the green foliage of even the worst affected plants.

Although bamboos will grow in poor-quality soils, their growth will inevitably be restricted as a result. There is no secret about it – bamboos need to be well fed in order to flourish. Although the nutrients they require occur naturally in the soil, they are not always present in sufficient quantities and it may be necessary to add a fertilizer (preferably organic) to reinvigorate the plant. One application should be made in February or March to stimulate the growth of young shoots, and another in July to August to feed the rhizomes. An interim application can be made in June. The fertilizer should contain nitrogen (10 per cent), phosphoric acid (5 per cent) and potassium (5 per cent), and each application should be applied at 25–50 grams per square metre (1–2 oz per square yard), depending on the richness of the substrate.

If bamboo is compared to a tree, the rhizomes correspond to the trunk and branches, and the culms to the leaves. Every year, the rhizomes produce more lateral branches and the culms, like the leaves, develop rapidly, producing new annual growth which withers and dies at the end of the season without affecting the main plant. Unlike the trunk and branches of a tree, the rhizomes grow below ground with only the "foliage" (the culms) visible. It is worth taking a closer look at the rhizomes, because their structure and growth habit determine the general appearance and habit of the plant.

The growth of some rhizomes is monopodial, which means they elongate from the tip of the main axis of growth and give rise to lateral branches. In other rhizomes, growth is sympodial: that is, they do not grow from the tip but from a system of lateral buds and branches. Rhizomes that grow sympodially are usually short and soon turn upwards, a phenomenon known as negative geotropism. As soon as the terminal bud emerges from the soil, it grows into a culm, which is why the lateral buds – and not the tip – are the main axis of growth. However, since the lateral buds also emerge from the soil and grow into culms, sympodial rhizomes always produce bamboos that grow in tightly packed clumps, known as cespitose* bamboos.

The rhizomes of running bamboos grow monopodially, which means they run horizontally beneath the surface of the soil and, when they emerge, either grow back into the soil or quite often, like their sympodial counterparts, grow into culms. As a result, the culms emerge at irregular intervals from some of the rhizome's lateral buds, which explains why they are fairly widely spaced, with the bamboo spreading as the rhizomes "run" through the soil.

Bamboos are usually either cespitose (clumping) or running, but some (*Shibataea kumasasa*) have mixed (sympodial and monopodial) rhizomes and are known as intermediates. A running bamboo can also sometimes grow in a compact clump, for example *Phyllostachys viridis* when it is planted in a cold climate. The soil cools down earlier than in a warmer climate, the growth of the rhizomes is restricted and the plant remains cespitose. Most temperate bamboos are running, while the tropical varieties are cespitose. In evolutionary terms, the cespitose bamboos are the ancestors of the running bamboos.

Bamboos are an asset to any garden: graceful, arching stems that add a touch of elegance, the freshness of evergreen leaves, the sound of the wind rustling through their leaves and, in summer, areas of cool shade created by the taller varieties. But they also add another dimension, an almost spiritual quality that introduces a note of peace and tranquillity – and Oriental magic – into the garden.

*Arundinaria sp.** (x 0.5)

This particular *Arundinaria* was recently imported from China. As the plant is not yet fully grown, it has so far been impossible to determine its species. The first indication is its glossy, orange-yellow rhizome.

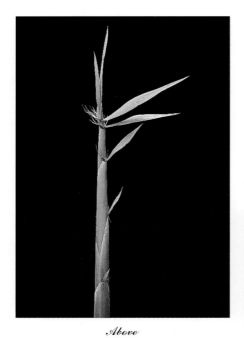

Above

Arundinaria funghomii (shoot)

The very straight, bright green culms of this bamboo produce clusters of erect and relatively undivided branches.

Chusquea culeou (turion) (x 2)

This native of Chile has erect culms, densely covered with clusters of short, leafy branches around the nodes. The pale colour of the young shoots provides a striking contrast to the dark green foliage.

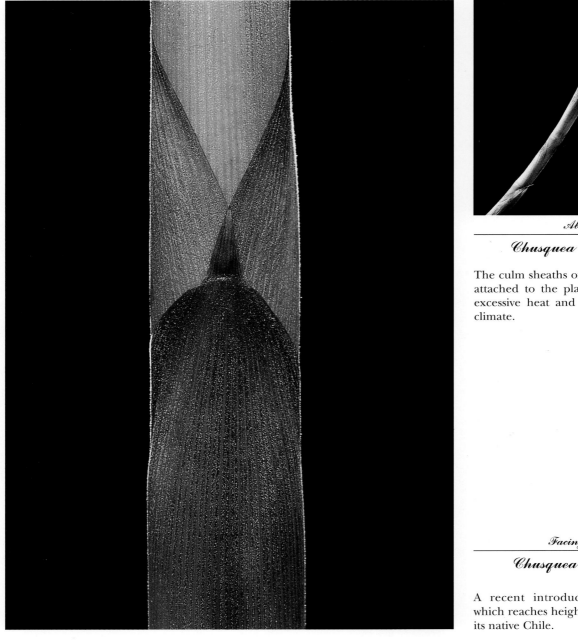

Above

Chusquea culeou (x 0.3)

The culm sheaths of this species remain attached to the plant. It does not like excessive heat and thrives in a coastal climate.

Facing page

Chusquea quila (x 0.3)

A recent introduction into Europe, which reaches heights of 15 m (49 ft) in its native Chile.

Drepanostachyum falcatum (x 1)

This cespitose bamboo, with its particularly fine and elegant foliage, grows to a height of between 3 and 4 m (10–13 ft). If it were slightly more frost resistant – it only withstands temperatures above – 5°C (23°F) – it would be found in gardens and on terraces, patios and balconies throughout Europe.

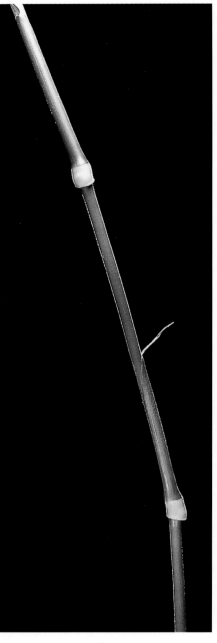

Above

Dinochloa scandens (young shoot)
(x 0.5)

Botanists disagree on the classification of this species. Whatever their opinion, it is basically a climbing bamboo that supports itself on the larger trees in its native tropical forest.

Hibanobambusa tranquillans (turion) (x 0.8)

This native of Japan grows to a height of between 2 and 3 m (6–10ft). It is probably a natural hybrid of *Sasa* and *Phyllostachys*, two very different genera. *Sasa* are usually small, large-leaved bamboos, while *Phyllostachys* are tall with small leaves. This attraction of opposites has produced a very pleasing result.

Hibanobambusa tranquillans
'Shiroshima' (x 1.5)

As well as having attractively variegated foliage, this cultivar also remains totally unaffected by extremely hard frosts.

Hibanobambusa tranquillans
'Shiroshima' *(young shoot)* (x 0.5)

The culms of the cultivar are not quite as tall as those of the type specimen. The tip of the young shoots is a delicate shade of pink.

Hibanobambusa tranquillans
'Shiroshima' (x 0.5)

A frost- and drought-resistant cultivar. Like many other bamboos, when the plant is short of water its leaves curl to reduce evaporation.

Himalayacalamus sp. (turion) (x 0.7)

As its name suggests, this genus is a native of the Himalayas, where it grows at altitudes of between 1,800 m (5,900 ft) and 2,500 m (8,200 ft) in well-watered conditions. It is therefore frost resistant but does not tolerate drought. All its species are cespitose bamboos and most produce edible shoots.

Phyllostachys aurea
(turion a few days old)
(x 1.1)

Although these young culm sheaths are
still fulfilling their protective function,
they soon begin to dry out at the edges.

Phyllostachys aurea (shoot)
(x 0.7)

A species found widely in Europe, characterized by the deformed internodes
on the lower part of some of the culms.
These internodes, which sometimes
resemble those of *Ph. pubescens heterocycla*
and sometimes those of *Bambusa ventricosa*, often form a chaotic sequence without any apparent order or governing
principle.

Indocalamus latifolius (x 0.2)

This small bamboo is widely used in China for making pen-holders, chopsticks, hats, and mats.

Facing page

Phyllostachys arcana
'Luteosulcata'

This cultivar is widely used as an ornamental bamboo due to its yellow sulcus* (internodal groove), which provides a striking contrast to the green of the culm.

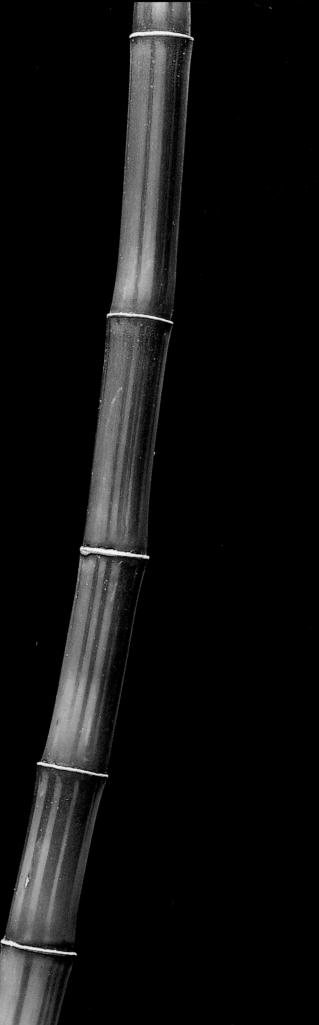

Himalayacalamus hookerianus
'Damarapa' (x 2)

The type specimen grows in the Himalayas at altitudes of between 2,000 m (6,500 ft) and 2,500 m (8,200 ft). Its wood is widely used in basket-making and its leaves as animal fodder. The culms of *H. hookerianus* 'Damarapa' have yellow striations.

Phyllostachys aurea
'Albovariegata' (x 1.3)

This extremely decorative green and white foliage is rarely found in the *Phyllostachys* genus. Seen from a distance, it gives the plant a silvery appearance. (*Ph. aurea* 'Albovariegata' began flowering in 1994 but is currently out of cultivation in Europe.) Flowering was provided by David Cramptom, holder of the National Collection of Bamboos (GB).

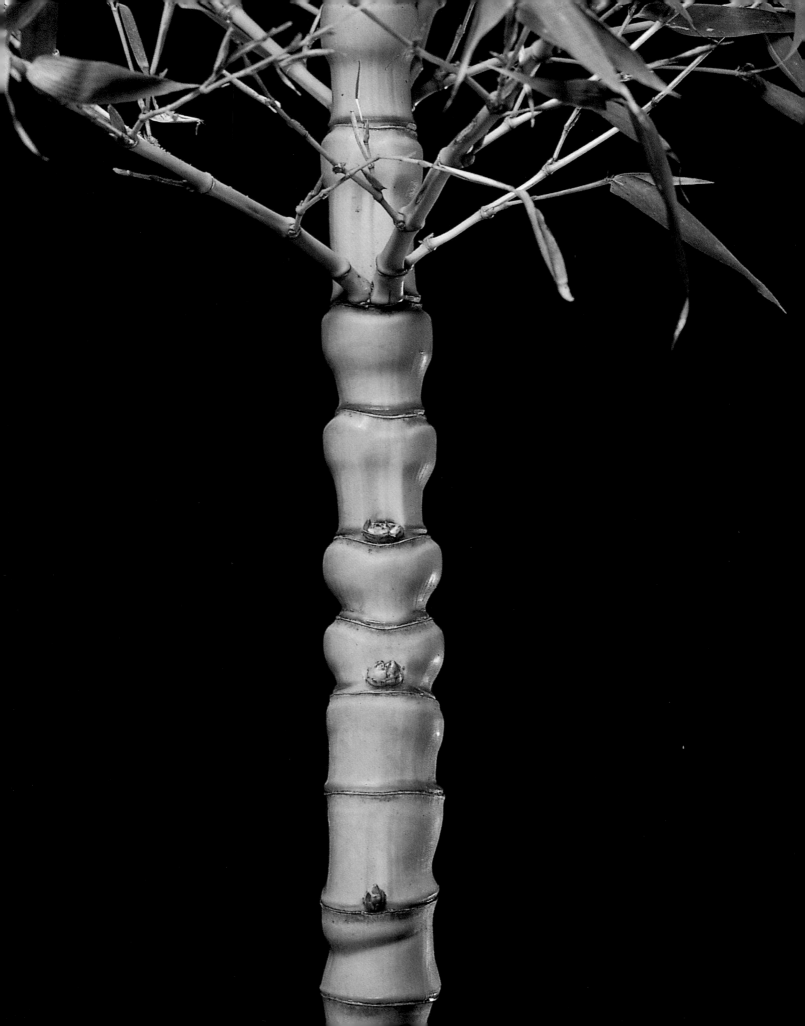

Phylloslachys aurea
'Holochrysa' (x 1.5)

The occasional leaf is discreetly marked with one or two whitish striations.

Phylloslachys aurea
'Holochrysa' (x 1.2)

More golden (*aurea*) than the type specimen since its culms and branches are yellow, whether or not they are exposed to sunlight. In the type specimen, only the parts of the plant exposed to the sun turn yellow.

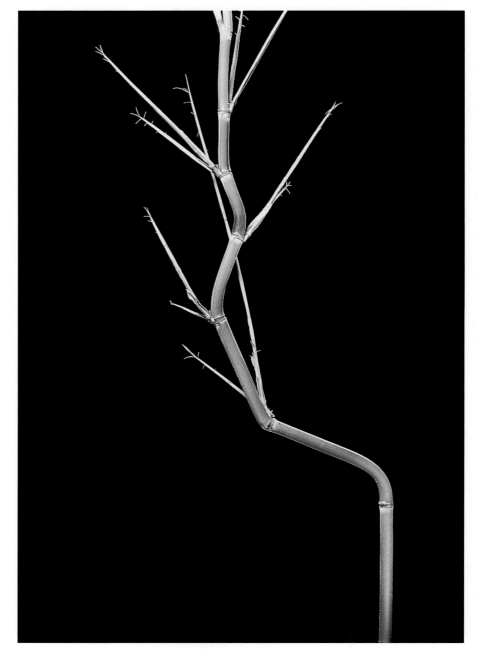

Right

Phylloslachys aureosulcala (young shoot) (x 0.3)

As its name suggests, this species has a golden-yellow sulcus. It is decorative, edible, and extremely frost resistant, but does not tolerate wind. The bases of some of its culms grow in the form of a "zigzag" involving two or three internodes, and occasionally four, as shown here.

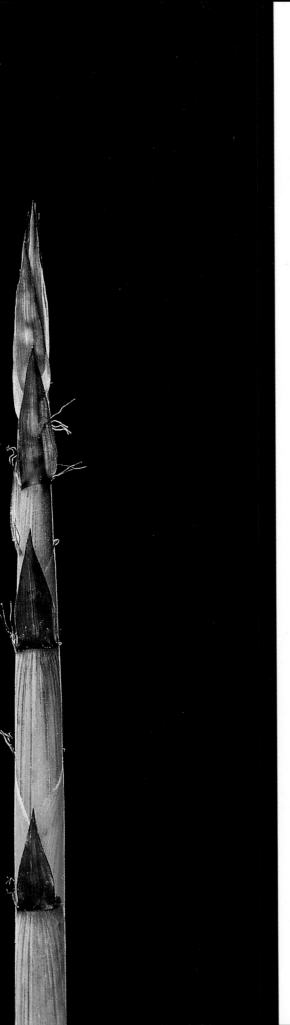

Phyllostachys aureosulcata
'Aureocaulis' *(turion)* (x 1.4)

The culm sheaths of this delicate turion are lightly striated. They become more heavily marked on the stronger culms.

Phyllostachys aureosulcata 'Aureocaulis' *(young shoot)* (x 1.5)

The culm of this cultivar is completely yellow, sometimes very finely striated with green. In spring, the young shoots are tinged with purple and the decorative effect is truly remarkable.

Phyllostachys aureosulcata
'Spectabilis' *(young culm)* (x 1.7)

The culm of the type specimen is green
with yellow striations. In the cultivar
'Spectabilis', it is yellow with green striations. The striations occur along the
sulcus, which means they appear alternately in the internodal sections of the
culm. The young shoots become tinged
with purple in the sun.

Phyllostachys aureosulcata **'Spectabilis'** *(sheath auricle)* (x 4.9)

The details of the various component elements of the culm sheath are vital in determining the species of a particular bamboo. Here the auricle* bordered by cilia* is clearly visible, although in this species it does not appear on the sheaths at the base or on the upper half of the culm.

Phyllostachys bambusoides *(turion)* (x 1.9)

The turions do not emerge from the ground until early summer. However, once they have emerged, they can grow as much as 1 metre (3 ft) in 24 hours!

Phyllostachys bambusoides (x 0.5)

This temperate giant is widely cultivated in China and Japan for the quality of its culms, which are used in the construction and craft industries. Sometimes the culms grow in the form of a more or less clearly defined "zigzag".

Phyllostachys bambusoides (shoot) (x 2.2)

The well-developed auricles of the culm sheaths are bordered by long cilia. The ligule* (the strap-shaped membranous outgrowth at the base of the sheath) is fimbrillate or "fringed".

Following double page, left

Phyllostachys bambusoides 'Holochrysa' *(young shoot)* (x 1.2)

The magnificent yellow culms of *Ph. bambusoides* 'Holochrysa' turn a particularly attractive shade of saffron yellow, depending on the amount of sunlight, soil type, and time of year.

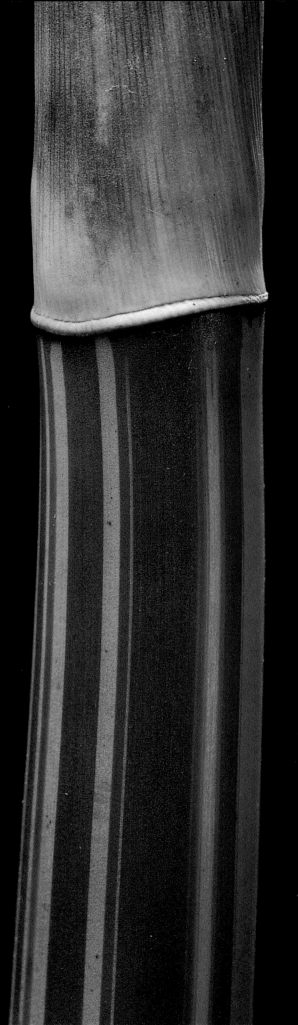

Bambusa multiplex
'Alphonse Karr'
(young shoot) (x 4.2)

Syn.: *Bambusa glaucescens* 'Alphonse Karr'.

Like all varieties of *B. multiplex*, this cultivar is cespitose, prefers hot climates, but will also tolerate temperatures as low as -9°C (16°F).

Although it is often referred to as *B. multiplex* 'Alphonso Karri', there are absolutely no grounds for this version of its name since it was named after the French writer Alphonse Karr.

Bambusa multiplex 'Fernleaf'
(x 0.7)

Syn.: *Bambusa glaucescens* 'Fernleaf'.
This cultivar is named after the form of
its leaves which, like the leaves of a fern,
are regularly and alternately spaced
along the branch. Closely related to
'Alphonse Karr', it is also cespitose and
frost resistant.

Bambusa ventricosa (x 1.4)

B. ventricosa is commonly known as
"Buddha belly" because, under certain
conditions, the internodes swell as the
shoots are growing, giving it the "pot-
bellied" appearance that makes it so attractive. Fortunately, it is also extremely
attractive when it is not swollen since a
bamboo bought in its "swollen" form
usually produces slender shoots.
It is a cespitose, tropical bamboo that
will, however, withstand temperatures as
low as -5°C (23°F).

Right

Bambusa ventricosa (x 0.5)

This young shoot has practically finished growing. The internodes are much shorter when swollen and reduce the overall height of the culm. The "ventricose" culms can be as much as two-thirds the height of the straight culms on the same plant.

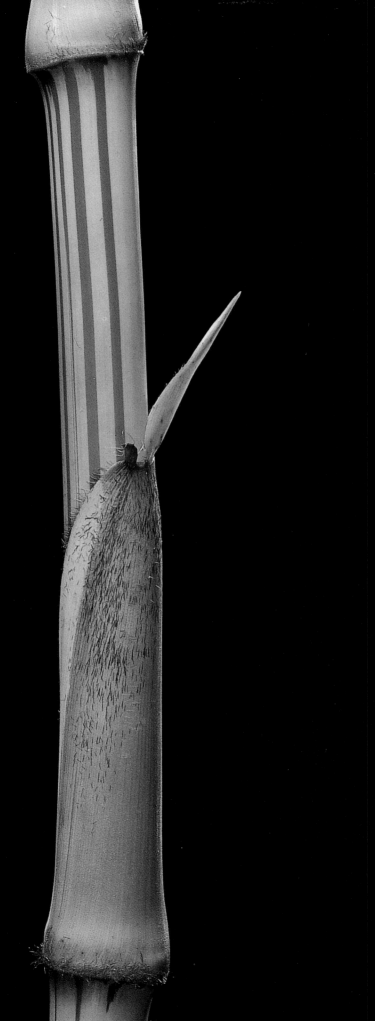

Bambusa vulgaris 'Vittata' *(young shoots)* (x 2.1)

The cultivar *B. vulgaris* 'Vittata', also known as *B. vulgaris* 'Striata', has an extremely attractive yellow culm with green striations. It is a cespitose bamboo that can grow to a height of over 20 m (65 ft), although it only does well in a tropical climate. The type specimen is so widely spread throughout the world that it is impossible to determine its origin. It should be handled with care as the sheaths that protect the young shoots are beautifully shiny and glossy on the inside, but on the outside covered with tiny brown hairs that irritate the skin.

Chimonobambusa marmorea (young shoots) (x 1.2)

Chimonobambusa means "winter bamboo". In western Europe, the young shoots develop in autumn and winter, and the leaves are produced in spring. *Marmorea,* meaning "marble", is a reference to the delicately marbled markings on the culm sheaths. The green culms turn varying shades of deep purple in autumn. The most striking culms are those of the cultivar *Ch. marmorea* 'Variegata', which are sometimes a cherry red colour and look really spectacular against the deep green of the foliage.

Chusquea coronalis

Ch. coronalis is a native of America that grows well only in hot climates. Around the nodes, short branches bear clusters of slender, delicate leaves. In its native tropical forest, the plant's fine, flexible culms use the branches of neighbouring trees for support.

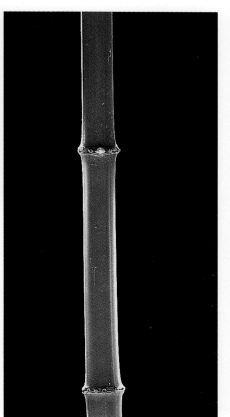

Above

Chimonobambusa quadrangularis (x 2)

Syn.: *Tetragonocalamus angulatus.*
This bamboo lives up to its genus name by producing its young shoots in winter, while the "quadrangular" culms account for its species name. The culms would in fact be more accurately described as circular and flattened on four sides, a characteristic that can best be ascertained by touch. The short branches grow in clusters from the nodes.

Right

Chimonobambusa quadrangularis (x 0.6)

The dense, pendulous foliage borne by the culms makes this an extremely elegant and impressive bamboo. It is much sought after in Japan as an ornamental plant for verandahs and small gardens, and is also used to make the calligraphers' brushes used by Buddhist monks.

Phyllostachys bambusoides
'Castilloni-inversa' *(turion)* (x 0.7)

The turions of the cultivars Holochrysa, Castillonis and Castilloni-inversa can be distinguished from those of the type specimen by the purple markings on their sheaths.

Phyllostachys bambusoides
'Castillonis'
(shoot) (x 0.5)

Its beautiful yellow culms, striated with green along the sulcus, place this cultivar among the ten most ornamental temperate bamboos.

Phyllostachys bambusoides
'Holochrysa' (x 1.4)

Occasionally, some of the culms have a fine green stripe on one or two of the internodes.

Phyllostachys bambusoides
'Castillonis' (x 0.8)

Although most of its leaves are entirely green, some are marked with fine white or pale yellow stripes.

Phyllostachys bambusoides
'Marliacea' (x 1)

A cultivar characterized by its "ribbed" internodes. These beautifully "inscribed" striations produce some remarkable decorative effects as the light changes. Certainly a bamboo to admire, and also to touch.

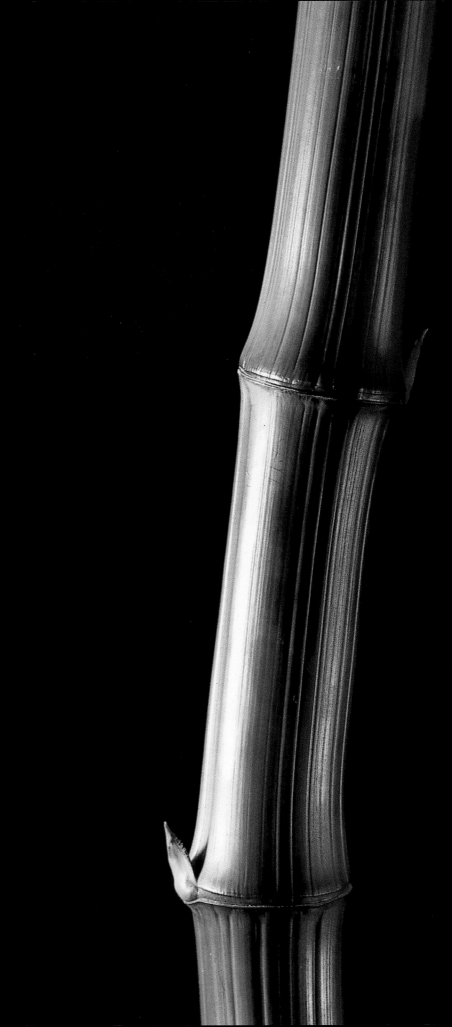

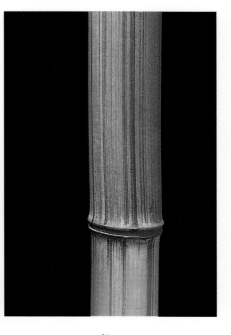

Phyllostachys bambusoides
'Violascens' (x 5.9)

The culms are striated with yellow,
orange, or brownish-mauve, depending
on their age.

Phyllostachys bambusoides
'Violascens' (x 0.5)

Some botanists classify this bamboo as a
cultivar of *Ph. bambusoides*, while others
consider it a species in its own right, in
which case it should be called *Ph. violascens*. The auricles on the leaf sheath have
particularly well-developed cilia.

The bamboos

54

Right

Phyllostachys decora
(young shoot) (x 0.7)

A name justified by its elegant foliage and the colour of the culms – yellowish-green tinged with orange – when exposed to the sun.

Facing page

Phyllostachys decora (x 2.1)

The culm sheaths are edged with purple at the tip and around the ligule.

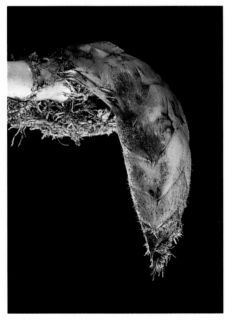

Phyllostachys pubescens (x 0.5)

The bud has clearly changed direction and will emerge from the soil in early April.

Phyllostachys pubescens (x 1.6)

The bud continues to grow, even in the depths of winter. It is swelling steadily and is already "fatter" than the rhizome from which it emerged.

Phyllostachys pubescens (x 0.5)

This turion is growing from a rhizome. The lighter areas – the rhizome and base of the turion – are underground. The turion emerges from the soil in April and is then ready to eat.

Above

Phyllostachys pubescens (x 0.2)

Four closely positioned buds have developed into turions. It is unlikely that the rhizome will have enough reserves to enable them all to grow into culms, and one will probably die a few days after emerging from the soil.

Phyllostachys pubescens (x 3.8)

These roots at the base of the turion are breaking through the culm sheaths and making their way into the soil, where they will ensure that the culm is firmly anchored and remains upright. In view of the extremely rapid growth rate of the culm, the roots must also develop quickly if they are to fulfil that function.

Phyllostachys pubescens (x 0.6)

The turion puts on new growth each day. Under certain conditions, it can grow more than 1 metre (3 ft) in 24 hours. Droplets of moisture secreted by the shoot drip from the tip of the limbs, creating the effect of rain, which looks particularly spectacular against a cloudless sky.

Phyllostachys pubescens (x 1.3)

The growth of the culm sheath is closely related to that of the internode. If a sheath is removed during the growth process, the internode simply stops growing, a technique used when creating bonsai.

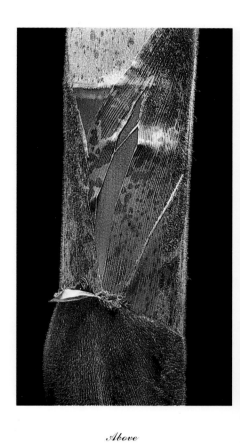

Phyllostachys pubescens (x 0.4)

When the inter-nodes have finished gro-wing, they no longer require the protec-tion of the culm sheaths, which dry up and are discarded by the culm.

Phyllostachys pubescens (x 0.8)

In Japan and China, the tough, fibrous culm sheaths are used to make sandals or wrap presents and sometimes food. Every part of the bamboo is used.

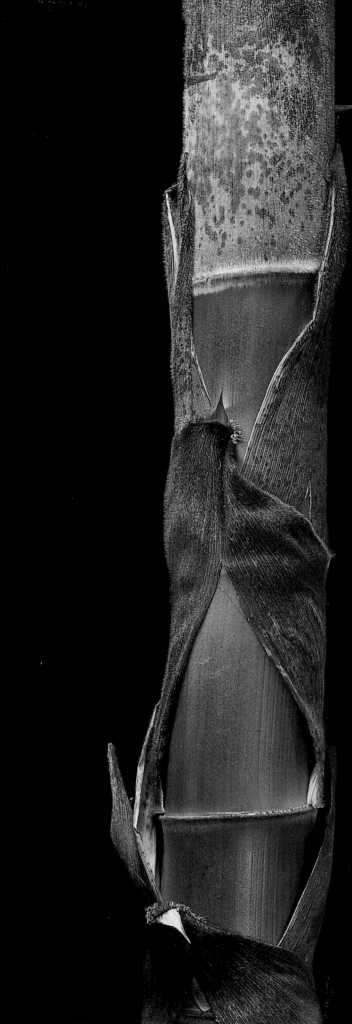

Phyllostachys pubescens (x 1.6)

Phyllostachys pubescens (x 0.6)

Although some roots have developed around the base of the culm and are already well established in the soil, others continue to develop. However, this is not a gratuitous proliferation of roots. Bamboo culms are not set deeply in the soil and these roots are all that keeps them upright. The new foliage will give the wind a much greater purchase on the culm, which will need all the anchorage available. The roots are so firmly attached to the inter-nodes at the base of the culm that, in China, they are used to make extremely strong brushes.

After the culm sheaths have been discarded, the culms of *Ph. pubescens* are covered in a powdery film rich in hormones. This bloom* has medicinal properties that accelerate the healing of wounds.

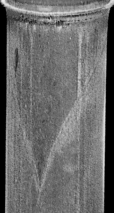

Phyllostachys pubescens (x 0.5)

The culm is fully grown within a few weeks, after which it does not increase in size or diameter. Its wood darkens with age and can be exploited after 4 or 5 years. Depending on the level of exposure to sunlight, the colour of the culms changes from bluish-green to golden-yellow.

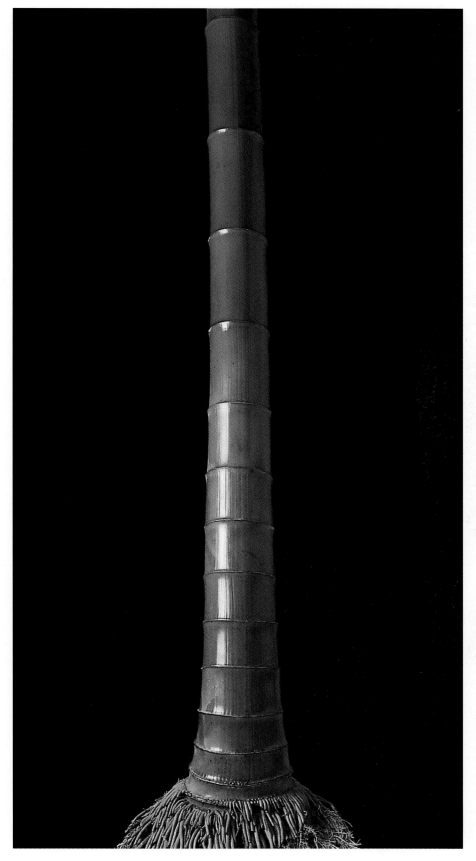

Phyllostachys pubescens (x 0.4)

The culm is fully grown and the basal roots are firmly anchored in the soil, ensuring that it remains upright. They will be put to the test by the force of the wind exerted on the foliage and branches and transmitted to the base of the culm via the 20 m (65 ft) lever of the stem. The culm is structured accordingly, with the short, compact internodes at the base designed to resist the high tensions and pressures, which can be as much as 30 tons.

Right

Phyllostachys pubescens 'Bicolor' *(shoot)* (x 1.3)

A particularly attractive mutation has produced a yellow culm with occasional green striations. Although it does not grow to the same size as the type specimen, it is still rated as one of the "giants", easily reaching heights of over 12 m (39 ft) and diameters of over 10 cm (4 in).

Above

Phyllostachys pubescens
'Bicolor' (x 0.5)

The mutation, clearly visible on the culm, also occurs less obviously on certain leaves, in the form of one or two white or yellow lines. However, it would be inaccurate to describe the leaves as "variegated" from these slight traces.

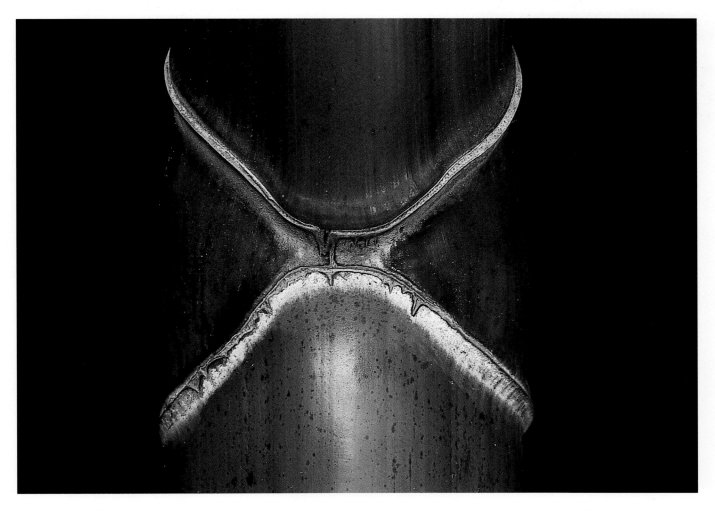

Phyllostachys pubescens heterocycla (x 0.3)

The internodes on the lower part of the culm are alternately swollen on one side and contracted on the other, giving this bamboo an unusual charm that makes it much sought after in Asia. It is also a very rare species that is extremely difficult to propagate. Seen from certain angles, it lives up to its Japanese name, *Kikko* (tortoiseshell).

Phyllostachys pubescens heterocycla (x 1.7)

In Asia, the culms of *Ph. pubescens heterocycla* are carefully preserved. They are highly prized for their magical powers and are often placed in shrines.

This modestly sized *Phyllostachys*, naturally 4 to 6 m (13–20 ft) in height, is widely used in Japan for creating bonsai. It is ideal for small to medium-sized gardens, especially for hedges or clumps of foliage.

Above

Phyllostachys incarnata (shoot) (x 0.5)

Ph. incarnata has bright reddish-brown culm sheaths flecked with brown. It is very popular in China for its edible shoots, which have a long growing period and a very high yield.

Left

Phyllostachys iridescens
(shoot) (x 1.3)

This species grows to heights of 8 to 12 m (26–39 ft). The culm sheaths are covered in a brownish-purple bloom, and the culms are more or less striated. It also produces delicious young shoots.

Phyllostachys meyeri (turion)
(x 0.8)

This *Phyllostachys* reaches a height of 8 to 9 m (26–30 ft). Its turions, and indeed the rest of the plant, are very much like those of *Ph. aurea*. The resemblance is so striking that some botanists are beginning to consider the possibility that *Ph. aurea* may be a mutation of *Ph. meyeri*, in which case they would both belong to the same species.

Above

Phyllostachys meyeri (shoot)
(x 1)

This particularly solid bamboo is widely used in the craft and construction industries.

Phyllostachys nidularia (turion) (x 1.5)

Ph. nidularia grows to between 6 and 8 m (20–26 ft) and, under certain conditions, to over 10 m (33 ft). The Chinese refer to it as the "bamboo with a turion in the form of a calligrapher's brush" and the "bamboo with big nodes". The internodes of most of the culms are solid, and the young shoots are truly delicious to eat. The wood, believed to release an odour that attracts prawns, is used for making hoop nets.

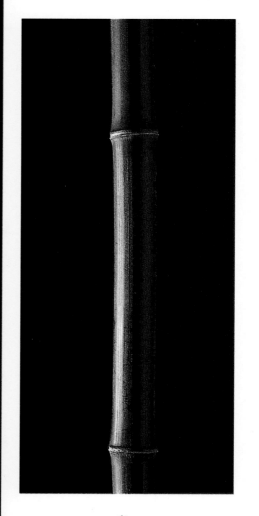

Above

Phyllostachys nigra (x 0.4)

The black colour of the culm and branches is particularly pronounced in regions where the plant is exposed to high levels of sunlight. However, if the plant is over-exposed to sun, the culms of *Ph. nigra* will in fact turn white.

Left

Phyllostachys nigra (turion)
(x 1)

Ph. nigra reaches a height of between 6 and 8 m (20–26 ft). Its turions are protected by sheaths covered with silky brown hairs, while the auricles develop long, reddish cilia. Over a period of three years, the young green culms gradually turn black, which is why it is called *nigra*. It looks beautiful in any garden, but should be given a position that is well sheltered from the wind.

Phyllostachys nigra 'Boryana'
(x 0.3)

Ph. nigra 'Boryana' is much stronger and more vigorous than *Ph. nigra*, and can reach heights of 12 to 18 m (40–60 ft). After the first year, the green culms become mottled with brown, yellow and chestnut, the intensity of the markings depending on the level of exposure to sunlight.

Phyllostachys nigra
'Boryana' *(turion)* (x 0.7)

All *Ph. nigra* have identical culm sheaths. Here, the limbs are crinkled because they were folded one against the other until the turion started to grow.

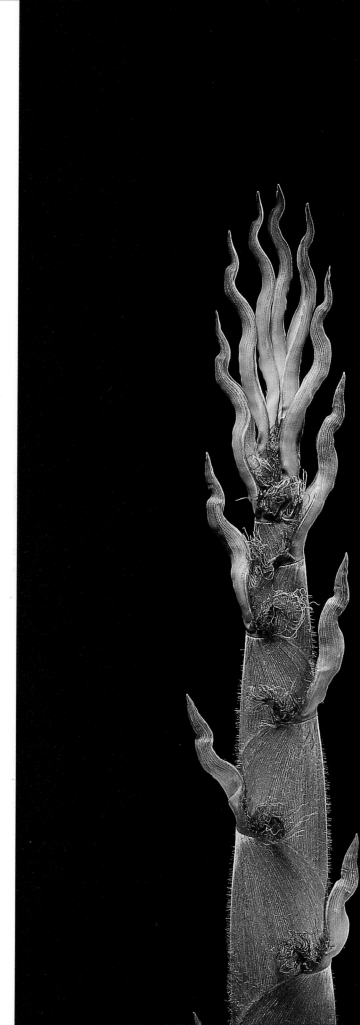

Phyllostachys nigra
'Boryana'
(detail of culm sheath) (x 1.5)

Although the sheaths are covered in hairs, they are quite safe to touch. Certain tropical bamboos, on the other hand, have nettling hairs that can cause an unpleasant skin reaction.

Phyllostachys nigra
'Henonis'
(turion) (x 0.6)

The green culms turn almost white if they are exposed to high levels of sunlight. This extremely frost- and drought-resistant bamboo can grow to a height of between 16 and 18 m (50–60 ft).

Phyllostachys nigra
'Henonis'
(turion) (x 2.2)

The sheath is typical of *Ph. nigra*. This bamboo, wrongly believed to be a cultivar or a variety of *Ph. nigra,* is in fact the type specimen from which *Ph. nigra* and *Ph. nigra* 'Boryana' were derived. Its name, which is misleading and – by present standards – inaccurate, is based on the old system of nomenclature.

Above

Phyllostachys nuda (turion)
(x 0.5)

The young culms of this bamboo, which grows to a height of 6 m (20 ft), are black and extremely decorative shortly after their sheaths have been discarded.

Right

Phyllostachys parvifolia (turion) (x 0.8)

The pale culm sheaths have lengthwise, yellow striations and are much lighter – almost white – towards the tip, below the base of the limb. There is a noticeable absence of auricles and cilia. *Ph. parvifolia*, which reaches a height of 6 m (20 ft), is grown for its edible shoots and its culms, which are divided into strips and used for making mats.

Phyllostachys propinqua (turion) (x 1)

There are no auricles or cilia on the pale culm sheaths, which are veined with red and have a purple ligule. This species, which reaches a height of 8 m (26 ft), is grown for the quality of its wood, used to make handles for tools and cut into strips for use in basketwork, as well as for its extremely tender young shoots.

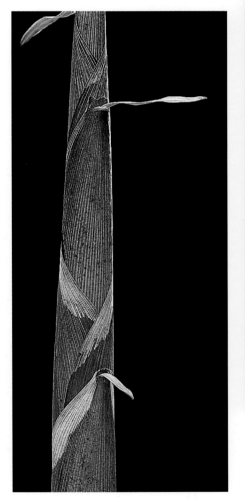

Phyllostachys viridiglaucescens (turion) (x 1)

Ph. viridiglaucescens grows to a height of 8 m (26 ft) and is extremely frost and drought resistant. When the culm sheaths are discarded, the bluish-green culms are covered in bloom, turning dark green after a year. It is used as a garden plant and for its young shoots and wood.

Phyllostachys viridis
'Houzeau' (x 0.3)

This bamboo is the result of a relatively frequent mutation that produces a yellow band in the sulcus of the green culms. The band is still present on the lower part of the culm, where the sulcus is less clearly defined.

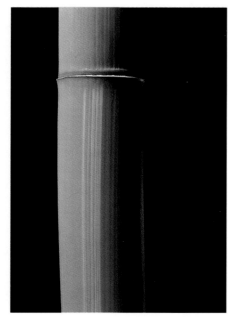

Above

Phyllostachys viridis (turion)
(x 0.5)

The turions of this 8 m (26 ft) bamboo emerge from the ground in late spring or early summer. Although some also appear sporadically in autumn, they often do not survive the winter. This truly delicious autumn crop is best harvested as soon as it appears.

Phyllostachys viridis
'Sulfurea' (x 0.5)

About the same size as *Ph. viridis*. A few months after the culm sheaths have been discarded, the pistachio green culms turn a bright, sulphur yellow (hence this bamboo's name).

Above

Phyllostachys viridis
'Sulfurea' (x 0.6)

The lower parts of some of the culms have green stripes that appear to have been painted onto the stems, making this an extremely popular ornamental plant.

Phyllostachys vivax (turion)
(x 1.2)

Ph. vivax grows to a height of 8 m (26 ft) and is virtually identical to *Ph. bambusoides.* However, the culm sheaths of *Ph. vivax* do not have auricles. The relatively thin wood is often cut into strips and used in basketwork.

This bamboo reaches a height of 3–4 m (10–13 ft). It has long, narrow leaves and its rhizomes grow deep down into the soil.

Pleioblastus chino '**Elegantissimus**' *(turion)* (x 0.5)

The culm sheaths, like the foliage, are striated with green and white. The intensity of the contrast varies with the seasons.

Above

Pleioblastus chino '**Elegantissimus**' (x 0.7)

Its mass of slender, variegated leaves gives this plant a "frothy" appearance that is unusual for a bamboo. Suitable for any garden, it can be planted as an individual specimen or used as an edging. It rarely grows above 3 m (10 ft).

Facing page

Pleioblastus distichus (x 1)

The leaves of this dwarf bamboo are regularly spaced on either side of the branch. Its dense and uniform habit makes it an ideal plant for bamboo "lawns".

Pleioblastus shibuyanus
'Tsuboï' (x 0.4)

A small bamboo, between 1.5 and 2 m (5–6 ft) in height, whose green leaves are marked with yellow along the central vein. These markings become less clearly defined and the contrast less intense as the leaf ages.

Below

Pleioblastus fortunei variegata
(x 1.1)

A dwarf bamboo whose downy leaves are strongly marked with green, yellow, and beige. It is ideal for stabilizing banks or for growing under trees.

Pleioblastus gramineus (shoot)
(x 0.7)

The dark green leaves of *P. gramineus* are long and slender, with a glossy upper surface. It forms compact, impenetrable clumps, 3 to 5 m (10–16 ft) high.

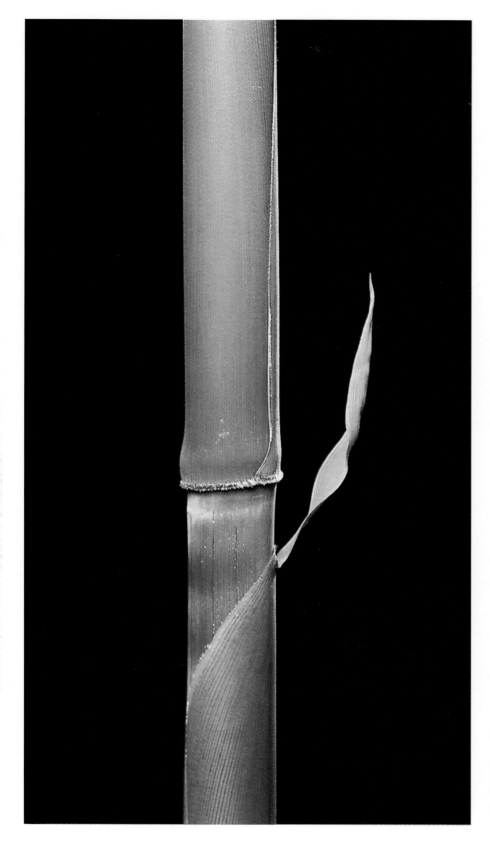

Left

Pleioblastus hindsii (young shoot) (x 0.9)

P. hindsii grows to a height of 5 to 6 m (16–20 ft). Its culms have relatively flat nodes and long internodes, which explains why its wood is so sought after for making flutes. Its young shoots are also much appreciated by gourmets.

Below

Pleioblastus viridistriatus
'Auricoma' (x 1.3)

Its superb yellow and green foliage is particularly bright in spring. The leaves are covered in tiny, silky hairs that make them velvety to the touch.

Right

Pleioblastus viridistriatus
'Chrysophyllus' (x 0.5)

The leaves, completely yellow in spring, become increasingly marked with green throughout the year.

Facing page

Pseudosasa japonica
'Akebono-suji' (x 1.1)

Although the leaves of the type specimen are completely green, the leaves of this cultivar are marked with beige, and the green is darker towards the tip.

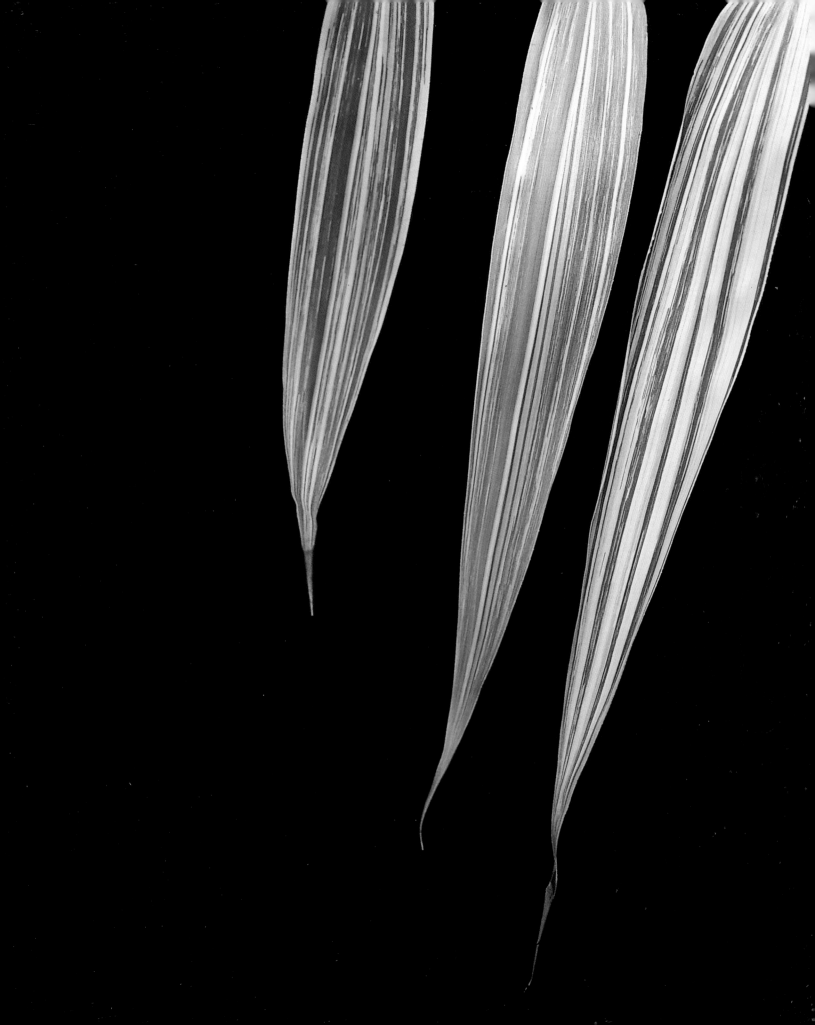

Pseudosasa japonica
'Tsutsumiana' (x 0.4)

This cultivar is smaller than the type specimen, it has a more compact habit, and its internodes are swollen at the base. It does not tolerate full sun.

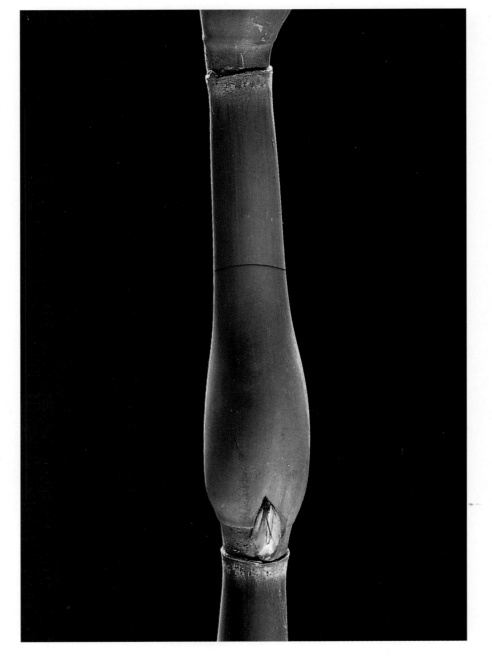

Above

Pseudosasa japonica
f. variegata (x 0.5)

A variegated form that is very similar to the 'Akebono-suji' cultivar, but which often reverts to type.

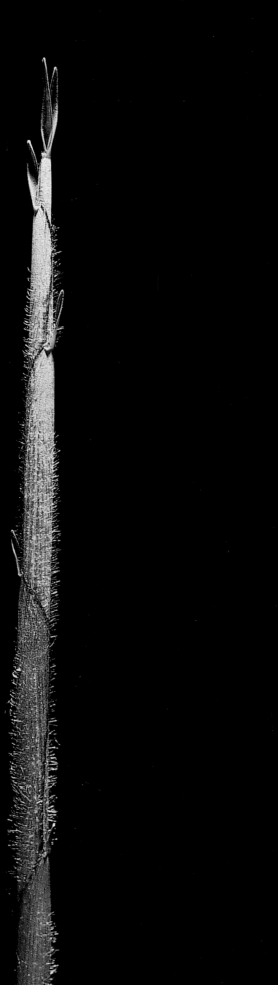

Sasa borealis (lurion) (x 1.6)

The culm sheaths of this bamboo are covered in long hairs. It is a native of Japan where it grows in regions liable to high snowfalls.

Sasa kurilensis (x 9.4)

This species grows wild in the northern mountains of the Japanese island of Honshu, where the local inhabitants are extremely fond of the young shoots, harvested in summer. The tessellated leaves (chequered division of the tissues between the veins) are an indication that the plant is extremely resistant to frost.

Sasa palmata nebulosa (x 0.3)

This species is named after the palm-like (*palmata*) arrangement of its broad, shiny green leaves at the end of the branch, and the dark grey, sometimes black, cloud-like (*nebulosa*) markings on the culms.

Sasa veitchii (x 0.6)

In winter, the cells around the edge of the leaves are killed by the cold. Although the leaves look fairly unattractive at close quarters, the overall effect is extremely decorative.

Left

Semiarundinaria fastuosa (turion) (x 0.3)

The turions emerge from the ground during late spring and early summer, sometimes even into autumn. The fastigiate (columnar) habit of the culms makes it an extremely ornamental plant, ideal for hedges.

Semiarundinaria fastuosa (x 0.7)

The glossy inner surface of the culm sheaths is tinged with an iridescent purple that gives it a shell-like appearance.

Semiarundinaria fastuosa (young shoot) (x 4.9)

The green outer surface of the culm sheath gives no indication of its beautiful shell-like interior.

Semiarundinaria fastuosa (x 0.5)

The green culms become tinged with purple in autumn, providing a striking contrast to their dark green foliage.

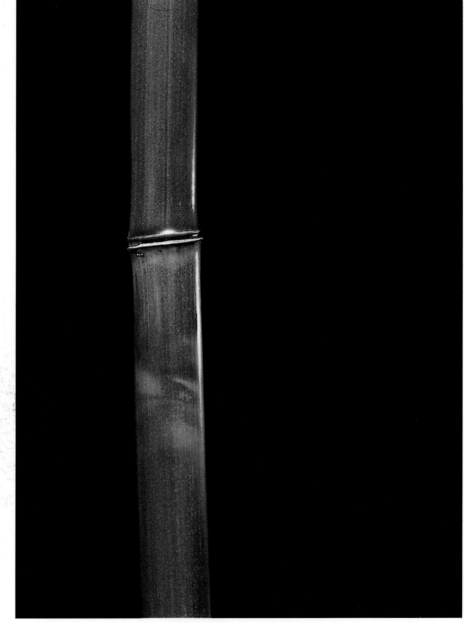

Semiarundinaria kagamiana
(x 1.6)

This native of Japan grows to a height of 4 to 5 m (13–16 ft). It thrives in all conditions and tolerates full sun and deep shade equally well.

Semiarundinaria yashadake
'Kimmei' (x 0.4)

Although the turions are less decorative than the culms, they do have attractively striated culm sheaths.

Facing page

Semiarundinaria yashadake
'Kimmei' *(turion)* (x 0.6)

As the culm sheaths are discarded, they reveal magnificent yellow culms with pink-tinged green striations. What is more, the culms turn scarlet if exposed to winter sunlight during their first year.

Above

Semiarundinaria kagamiana
(x 0.5)

The branches around the nodes bear dense clusters of leaves.

Right

Shibataea kumasaca (x 0.7)

Known as the "Ruscus-leaved bamboo" due to the shape of its leaves – even though the Ruscus doesn't have leaves but cladodes (flattened stems that act and look like leaves) – its evocative name makes it immediately recognizable. It is probably the best species for neatly trimmed edgings.

Facing page

Semiarundinaria yashadake 'Kimmei' (x 1.9)

Recently introduced and therefore still relatively unknown in Europe, its graceful elegance and beautiful culms will guarantee its success.

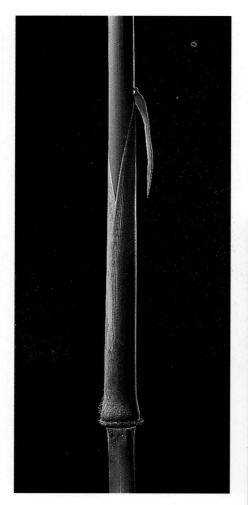

The culms, which grow to between 1.5 and 2 m (5–6 ft), are often solid and grey-green in colour. The lower part of each node is marked by a ring of white bloom.

Above

Sinobambusa tootsik (young shoot) (x 0.5)

Easily recognized by the red down at the base of the culm sheath. In Japan, the fastigiate (columnar) culms are often cut to accentuate its naturally "layered" habit.

Above

Yushania maling (x 2)

Found in the Himalayas at an altitude of
between 1,600 m (5,000 ft) and 3,000 m
(10,000 ft). The extremely rough culm is
rather like sandpaper.

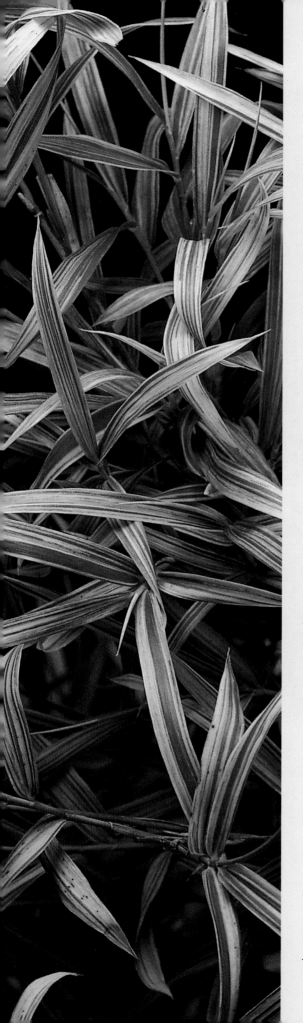

Bamboos in the garden

In the nineteenth century, Jules Cloquet of the Paris Zoological Society predicted that bamboo would be introduced into Europe via industrial channels: "Bamboo will one day be to industry what the potato is to the food sector". Others believed that, in France, it was more likely to appear on people's plates, given that country's great culinary tradition. It is somewhat surprising that such a delicious vegetable has continued to remain relatively unknown and under-valued in the West.

Bamboo in fact entered Europe via its gardens, but only relatively recently, with the first Phyllostachys nigra *arriving in England in 1827. Other species followed, mainly introduced by Eugène Mazel, who founded the famous park devoted to bamboos and other exotic plants at Prafrance, near Anduze in the French Cévennes region. This park became known as "La Bambouseraie", a name which conveys its truly unique character and which has since found its way into the French language where it is used (incorrectly) to refer to a plantation of bamboos.*

Although bamboos were used as ornamental plants in Europe in the late nineteenth and early twentieth century, the limited range available and the general lack of knowledge did little to increase their popularity. Since then, the selection has been greatly extended and gardeners now have a choice of one hundred or so different bamboos that can be used decoratively – planted in clumps, groups, or groves – or functionally to create "lawns", ground cover, edging, or hedges. The possibilities are as varied as the plants themselves.

Bamboo "lawns"

Bamboo "lawns" are created using dwarf bamboos, maintained at heights of between 5 and 25 cm (2–10 in), and have the major advantage of needing to be cut only once or twice a year. The first cut is carried out at the end of winter, to a height of 5–10 cm (2–4 in), using a lawn mower, strimmer, hedge-trimmer, or shears. The second cut is carried out, if necessary, in summer to trim any plants that have grown too tall. These "lawns" are extremely useful in areas that are relatively inaccessible and/or difficult to mow. In the case of banks, for example, they serve a dual purpose. The bamboo not only covers the ground, but its dense, strong rhizome system also serves to stabilize the soil, preventing landslides or excessive soil erosion. Although extremely pleasant to look at, bamboo "lawns" are not particularly user friendly when it comes to picnics or a quiet siesta, since their softly regular foliage conceals the equally regular but particularly unyielding culms.

To create a bamboo "lawn", the ground is prepared in the same way as for a traditional lawn and then planted with dwarf bamboos. The number of plants required depends on their vigour, and varies between three and sixteen plants per square metre (square yard). Plants are sold in pots or small containers.
Recommended varieties:
Green foliage: *Pleioblastus distichus, Pl. pumilis, Pl. viridistriatus* 'Vagans'.
Variegated foliage: *Pleioblastus fortunei, Pl. viridistriatus* 'Auricoma'.

Ground cover

The same varieties are used as for "lawns". However, bamboos used as ground cover are maintained differently since they do not have to be cut every year. They are simply required to cover the ground fairly evenly and keep down any unwanted plants and weeds.

Although evenness of height is not paramount, ground-cover bamboos can occasionally be cut back hard (for example every 8–10 years) to promote new growth. If cut up or shredded, the cuttings can be left on the ground as they make an excellent mulch and will eventually enrich the soil with organic matter. This type of ground cover can be grown under trees and shrubs, around ponds, on banks, along streams, in areas of scrubby vegetation, etc.
In addition to the varieties recommended for "lawns":
Green foliage: *Sasa masamuneana, Indocalamus tesselatus, S. tsuboiana, Shibataea kumasasa.*
Variegated foliage: *Sasa masamuneana* 'Albostriata'.
"Mixed" foliage (green in summer and bordered with creamy white in winter): *Sasa veitchii.*

Bamboo edging

Bamboo can also be used to edge a particular area of the garden and especially to border a pathway. Most dwarf and small bamboos are suitable for this purpose. It may be necessary to cut them back to the required height once a year, in May or June. The best way to do this is to wait until the young shoots have finished growing and cut back before the new foliage develops. This can be done with shears or a hedge-trimmer.

There is no need to worry about rhizomes if the edging is separating a lawn from a path. Neither of these areas will allow the bamboo to spread, because the lawn is repeatedly mown and the path is constantly used. However, if bamboo is used to edge areas planted with shrubs or perennials, the rhizomes will tend to "invade" the planted areas. The best solution is to install some form of "rhizome barrier" when planting the bamboo: extremely effective barriers made of thick polypropylene are now widely available. The bamboos should be set in a straight line, leaving a gap of 30–60 cm (1–2 ft) between each plant.

Recommended varieties:
Shibataea kumasasa, Pleioblastus viridis-triatus 'Vagans', *Pl. chino* 'Elegantissimus', *Pl. shibuyanus* 'Tsuboï', *Sasa veitchii*.

Bamboo hedges

A bamboo hedge is just a larger version of a bamboo border. The planting principle is the same as for borders and it is therefore wise to use some form of barrier to reduce the spread of unwanted rhizomes.

Bamboo hedges can be cut like any other hedge. However, since bamboos only grow for 2–3 months of the year, they should be cut at the end of their growing period. The hedge will then remain at the same height and thickness until the following year. Alternatively, hedges can be left to grow freely, although they should be thinned out every 3–4 years by removing the old culms that have dried out and lost their leaves.

It is best to avoid planting a hedge with a single species. As and when that species flowers, it may well lose part – if not all – of its foliage, with the result that the entire hedge could be weakened and even die. The best solution is to use two or three different species. Flowering will still occur, but will go virtually unnoticed unless both or all three species flower simultaneously, which is statistically highly improbable.

A hedge consisting of several different varieties can be plain or variegated. A plain hedge will combine similar varieties so that even an experienced eye will not be able to tell that it consists of different bamboos: for example *Phyllostachys nuda, Ph. bis-setii, Ph. angusta, Ph. decora, Ph. heteroclada, Ph. humilis, Ph. nidularia*.

A variegated hedge is obtained by combining varieties with different coloured culms. For example, green culms (the list is endless) can be combined with yellow culms (*Ph. viridis* 'Sulfurea', *Ph. bambusoides* 'Holochrysa', *Ph. aurea* 'Holochrysa'), black culms (*Ph. nigra*), mottled culms

(*Ph. nigra* 'Boryana', *Ph. bambusoides* 'Tanakae'), striated culms (*Ph. bambusoides* 'Violascens') or two-tone culms (*Ph. bambusoides* 'Castillonis', *Ph. bambusoides* 'Castilloni-inversa', *Ph. aureosulcata*, *Ph. aureosulcata* 'Spectabilis').

Apart from being extremely beautiful to look at, bamboo hedges also make very good wind-breaks and can block out noise.

Clumps of bamboo

Clumps of bamboo are ideal for creating the impression of a solid feature and can be used to fill and "decorate" a space, to soften lines, as a focal point and sometimes even to conceal the more unsightly aspects of a garden. For example, a compost heap can be successfully screened by a few clumps of *Sasa palmata* or *Fargesia nitida*, which are generously covered in foliage throughout the year. Clumps can also be used as a backdrop to emphasize form and colour. A few bamboos judiciously planted on the edge of a pond or pool will provide the added dimension of their reflected image on the surface of the water.

Bamboo groves

A bamboo grove is a bigger version of a clump. Any of the medium-sized and tall – or giant – varieties can be used to create a bamboo grove large enough for a person to walk into or through, or somewhere to sit and reflect beneath the culms. Groves can consist of a single species: although flowering may still occur, it does not present the same problems as for a hedge, which is usually more functional. They can also consist of sev-eral species. The skill of the landscape designer who chooses the combination of varieties and different coloured culms is complemented by that of the gardener who decides which culms to keep and which to remove when thinning out the plants. But this can be done in the knowledge that any mistakes will be remedied by the following year's growth. A bamboo grove, by its very nature, creates an area of physical and visual movement that changes and evolves over the years.

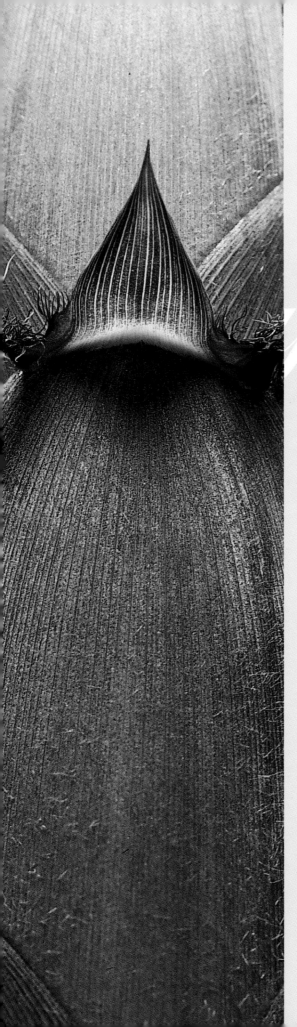

It would be more botanically correct to refer to "fields" rather than "forests" of bamboo. Like "grove", "forest" is a term usually applied to trees and, as has already been established, bamboos are not trees.

In 1906, the Belgian botanist and bamboo specialist Jean-Auguste Hippolyte Houzeau de Lehaie described a bamboo "forest" in his journal *Le Bambou*: "It is difficult for anyone who has not lived in the tropics to imagine the true majesty of a bamboo forest. There are not many in Europe and Prafrance is one of the few places where the sheer size and vigour of these truly magnificent plants can be fully appreciated.

"... Imagine hundreds of stems: here in serried ranks, shooting skywards like rockets, there regularly spaced and, a little further on, in twos and threes, like little groups of walkers. All are tall and slender, yet resilient, and the golden branches and green foliage of their summits are like tall parasols swaying gently in the breeze... These huge ostrich-plumed culms often grow to heights of 20 m (65 ft) or more, competing with some of the tallest trees in the forest. Nor are they daunted by the inclement European climate. Last year, Prafrance experienced the type of weather usually reserved for more northerly latitudes. Three days of gales, from 1 to 3 January 1905, were followed by heavy snows and temperatures that plummeted to -14°C (7°F). The snow had to be shaken from the tall culms, which were bent beneath its weight and in danger of breaking. But when the storm had subsided and the snows had melted, to everyone's great joy it was clear that not a single leaf had been damaged. The plants had withstood the cold remarkably well and were as vigorous as if the mild winter of southern France had not been interrupted by this interlude of northern gales."

Although bamboo "forests" are, of necessity, composed of "giant" species, some modestly sized varieties can also be used very successfully.

The "giants" that grow well in Europe are: *Phyllostachys bambusoides* 'Castillonis', *Ph. makinoi*, *Ph. nigra* 'Boryana', *Ph. nigra* 'Henonis', *Ph. pubescens*, *Ph. viridiglaucescens*, *Ph. viridis*, *Ph. vivax*, *Ph. viridis* 'Sulfurea'.

Bamboo in the vegetable garden

Fresh bamboo shoots are a prime vegetable. They are constructed rather like an onion, although the likeness ends there since they have neither the onion's consistency nor its taste. They contain germanium, believed to slow down the ageing process of cells. The young shoot or turion looks rather like an artichoke. The external leaves (sheaths) are tough and fibrous, while the internal leaves are crisp and tender. The edible part of the shoot accounts for 75–80 per cent of its total weight, which varies according to the species and method of culture. *Phyllostachys pubescens* produces the largest shoots cultivated in temperate climates, sometimes weighing as much as 2 kg (4½ lb). The turions are harvested in the morning, preferably as their tips emerge from the ground, by cutting them from the plant about 20 cm (7½–8 in) below the surface of the soil. It is rather like harvesting asparagus, but less tedious and much faster.

Bamboos in containers

Bamboos are not just plants for vast areas. They can be grown in small gardens, in containers on balconies, terraces, and verandahs, and even as houseplants.

A few precautions should be taken, however, when growing bamboos in containers, as this automatically means that they will have a limited amount of soil. The first thing to remember is that good drainage is paramount, so that the plant does not become waterlogged. This is easily achieved by ensuring that there are drainage holes in the container, and also by covering the bottom with a 5–6 cm (2–2½ in) layer of gravel, grit, or crocks. A piece of garden felt will prevent the finer particles of soil from clogging up the drainage layer.

If the container is part of a structure (balcony or terrace), its sides will be waterproof and the drainage water will be channelled away from the building. If it is well sealed, it will not be affected by the roots and rhizomes of the plant. However, a rhizome barrier can still be placed inside the container to provide added protection and should be inclined at an angle of 15° to the vertical. A mixture of wet sand and cement can be used to create a "lining" between the edge of the container and the barrier, so that any rhizomes that have not been cut back will be forced to change direction and emerge from the soil, where they may form new culms.

The soil should be light and well drained, but also be water retentive and contain a high level of nutrients. A mixture of peat-based compost (85 per cent), composted bark (10 per cent) and grit (5 per cent) suits most bamboos. They should also be fed regularly with a complete fertilizer that provides them with a slow release of nitrogen.

The depth of the container should correspond to the type of bamboo to be planted. Dwarf species will be happy in a container 40 cm (15 in) deep, small bamboos need a depth of 50 cm (20 in), medium-sized bamboos need 60–70 cm (24–28 in), while giant species must have a minimum depth of 80 cm (32 in). The height of medium-sized and giant bamboos will depend on the amount of soil available to the roots. For example, a bamboo 8–10 m (26–33 ft) high will live for 2–3 years in a container of 1 cu m (35 cu ft) but, with the best will – and care – in the world, it will be too restricted to do really well. The volume of the container (in cubic metres) should ideally be equal to half the desired height. For example, a 6 m (20 ft) *Phyllostachys* requires 3 cu m (106 cu ft) of soil in a container 80 cm (32 in) deep. This represents a surface area of 7.5 sq m (81 sq ft), which is equivalent to a square whose sides measure 2.75 m (9 ft) or a circle with a dia-meter of almost 3 m (10 ft).

Bamboos in the conservatory

All temperate and many tropical bamboos do well under glass, although the taller varieties will obviously have limited "head room". To avoid such problems, they should be grown in relatively small containers, fed sparingly and, if ne-cessary, the stronger-looking turions should be cut out as soon as they appear.

Most bamboos will thrive in these conditions, except in summer when the heat generated in a conservatory can be excessive, and there is a serious risk of burnt foliage. If possible, plants should be moved outside over the summer.

Bamboos in the house

Although bamboos make striking houseplants, it is difficult to achieve satisfactory results in the long term. It is, quite simply, impossible to provide ideal growing conditions for most temperate bamboos in an indoor environment. If they do not receive sufficient (2,000 lux minimum) and – ideally – zenithal light, the plants will gradually grow towards the light source, which will disturb their natural balance. Most temperate bamboos also need a period – usually provoked by colder temperatures – during which growth slows down, and few people would be prepared to turn off their central heating for 3 months in winter for the sake of their bamboos! Another problem is the lack of humidity, which causes the edges of the leaves to dry out. As well as being unsightly, this also upsets the natural processes of absorption and development. Plant sprays can solve the problem, but a fairly sophisticated system is required. The best temperate bamboos to grow as houseplants are:

Phyllostachys bambusoides 'Castillonis', *Ph. bambusoides* 'Castilloni-inversa', *Ph. nigra* 'Boryana', *Ph. nigra* 'Henonis', *Pseudosasa japonica*, *Semiarundinaria kagamiana*.

Tropical species that tolerate a relatively high year-round temperature generally do better as houseplants, although they too need adequate light and humidity. Current research should soon produce a bamboo that is better suited to an indoor environment.

Propagating bamboos

Propagation is almost always carried out vegetatively, that is, by removing and replanting part of an existing plant.

Culm cuttings produce good results only when taken from tropical bamboos, while rhizome cuttings are an ideal way to propagate temperate species. The process involves removing a section of rhizome that is about 3 years old and which includes at least three buds. The cutting should be planted at a depth of 15 cm (6 in) and watered in. After a few weeks, one or two delicate turions will emerge from the soil, as the rhizomes and roots develop beneath the surface. Cuttings should be taken a few days before the turions emerge, a time which will vary according to the species.

Choosing and planting bamboos

The first things to consider before choosing a bamboo are its end use (whether it is intended for a "lawn", a clump, a hedge, or an edging) and the ultimate height required. Having chosen a bamboo, it should be borne in mind that giant and many medium-sized bamboos will not achieve their ultimate height if they do not have ideal growing conditions (climate, soil, and care). The choice of bamboo will also be influenced by personal taste and the species' ability to adapt to the particular location and conditions under which it will be grown.

A high-quality bamboo will have a high number of rhizomes in the container, that is, in the clump. The rhizomes contain the reserves for the following year's growth. Although the visible part of the plant is important (it should look healthy and well balanced), it should not be taken as the sole indication of the quality of the plant. Many amateurs have been misled by apparently perfect-looking plants produced by unscrupulous or incompetent nurserymen who have removed clumps of bamboo from established groups, and grown them on in a container for only a few months before selling them. The results are bound to be disappointing as the freshly severed plants have to re-establish their own root and rhizome system before they can flourish, which may take them 2–3 years.

There are three possible, and equally accurate, answers to the question: "How old is this bamboo?" If referring to a specific culm, it is the age of that culm, calculated from the point at which the turion emerged from the ground. A culm is rarely more than 20 or 30 years old. If the question refers to an entire group, then the age is calculated from the time the group was planted, and added to the age of the original bamboo from which it developed. However, this calculation is fairly unsatisfactory (if not impossible) since bamboos are generally propagated vegetatively, that is, by the removal of an aerial and/or underground section of the parent plant. The biological age of the plant should technically be calculated from the point of germination of the seed that produced the first parent plant. As this parent plant will have been subsequently divided into a multitude of plants (known collectively as a clone), it is not always easy to trace a plant back to its origins. Biologically speaking, a bamboo – even if it has just been planted and is not particularly well developed – can be several decades, or even centuries, old.

A few basic principles of physiology will help to clarify the question of the development, and therefore the age, of a bamboo.

Imagine a plant belonging to a "giant" species that was propagated by vegetative division 2 years ago and has since been grown in a plastic pot. Its vegetative age is therefore 2 years, whereas its biological age may be much greater, even though its culms are barely 1 m (3 ft) high. If this bamboo is planted in the ground, its roots and rhizomes will quickly produce turions the following spring.

As soon as they emerge from the ground, the diameter of these turions will exceed that of the existing culms. After 8–10 weeks, the turions will have become mature culms with fully developed branches and foliage. Although similar in appearance to the existing culms, the new culms will be thicker and taller. This process will be repeated each year for the next 4–10 years, depending on the species and growing conditions. At the end of this period, the group will be fully mature and the new culms will no longer be thicker and taller, but have the same height and diameter as the previous year's culms. However, the plant will still not be entirely homogeneous as there will always be a few turions that are less well fed than the rest and which produce culms of below average size.

While the plant is re-establishing itself, between being planted and achieving full maturity, the thickest and tallest culms are therefore the youngest, a fact that has confused more than one amateur enthusiast. Bamboo physiology is the only explanation for this apparent contradiction.

According to Sato Shingen, "A clump of bamboo tended by one man takes ten years to become established; but a clump tended by ten men becomes established in a year".

Chinese popular tradition has a similar saying: "It takes one man ten years to create a forest of bamboo, while ten men can create the same forest in a year".

Both sayings illustrate the importance (weightiness in the literal and figurative sense) of the role played by the underground part of the plant in the future development of the group. Current techniques in container growing have made it possible to reduce the amount and weight of the growing medium to the advantage of the rhizomes, thereby increasing the underground reserves. A modern version of the Japanese and Chinese sayings would be: "One man can create a forest of bamboo in five years".

In fact, one man could easily plant bamboos grown in 15 litre (3¼ gallon) containers, whose weight would be in the region of 15 kg (33 lb). The bamboos, between 1.5 and 2 m (5–6 ft) tall when planted, would reach a height of between 8 and 12 m (26–40 ft) after 5 years, thus creating a forest. It would also be possible for five men to create a forest in 1 year since well-established container-grown bamboos, between 8 and 12 m (26–40 ft) tall and weighing 250–300 kg (550–660 lb), could be planted by five strong men. Whatever the size of the container, the method is the same.

The soil should ideally be prepared in advance and any stones, roots, and weeds removed. For dwarf bamboos, the soil need only be dug over to a depth of 25–30 cm (10–12 in). For other types, it is better dug to a depth of 35–40 cm (14–16 in). Add manure to the soil during this preparation stage, preferably well-rotted farmyard manure, 10–20 kg (22–44 lb) per square metre (square yard).

The plant should be well watered before being removed from its pot, if necessary by immersing it in a bucket of water for 5–10 minutes. It may also be necessary to cut the container to remove the plant as the swollen rhizomes (a sign of vigorous growth) often prevent it from being "turned out".

Once out of its pot, the bamboo can be planted. The bottom and sides of the hole to which the manure (or fertilizer) has been added should be loosened with a spade or pickaxe. The plant should then be placed in the hole so that the top of the root ball is level with the surface of the soil. Once the loose earth has been filled in and firmed down around the plant, the earth left over from the hole can be used to form a ridge around the plant and create a "basin" that will prevent water draining away and keep the roots well watered. The root ball should be well watered during and immediately after planting to give the plant the best possible start. There is no need to stake plants under 2.5 m (8 ft), but it is advisable to stake plants over this height for between 6 and 8 months until the root and rhizome system has become firmly established.

With regard to planting times, container-grown bamboos can be planted at more or less any time of the year with a good chance of success. However, a bamboo planted in open ground will have the best opportunity of becoming well established at the end of summer, when the soil temperature is ideal for the growth of the roots and rhizomes, which are then also at their most active.

Planting at the end of summer or the beginning of autumn will allow a bamboo to establish itself and be bet-ter able to withstand the rigours of winter, especially if protected by a mulch. Spring is less favourable for planting as the bamboo is being placed in relatively cold soil and is less likely to be able to establish itself rapidly. This is also the period when the plant has to support the growth of young shoots, and needs plenty of water and a great deal of care to ensure that it grows successfully.

Everyday maintenance of bamboos

Maintenance varies according to the type and variety of bamboo. Dwarf bamboos should be regularly cut back to ground level every 1–3 years. This is done to remove old culms and rejuvenate the foliage. It also gives the plant a more compact and uniform habit.

Small bamboos do not need to be cut, but simply "contained" in terms of height and spread if they become too invasive. Since cutting out old, dead culms is never very easy, it is simpler to cut the plant back hard at the end of winter. This will re-invigorate the plant and can be done every 5–10 years. If done more often it will reduce the size of the bamboos.

Medium-sized and giant bamboos should ideally be thinned out every year, or at least every 2–3 years, to remove the culms that have dried out or are nearing the end of their active life. This process makes it possible to remove any culms over 5 years old, always taking account of the appearance of the plant. By thinning out certain areas and leaving others more densely planted, the cutter can create a "rhythm" and "sculpt" the plant.

All types of bamboo need to be well watered if affected by dry weather or drought. The amount of feeding depends on the richness of the soil and the type of growth required. For example, a hedge that has reached the required height and density does not need to be fed every year. The same principle applies for clumps, groves, and any other combinations or arrangements of bamboo.

Glossary

Abbreviations

sp. : species, the subdivision of a genus or main plant group.
f. : form.

Auricle: an ear-like appendage that occurs at the base of some leaves.

Bloom: the fine, waxy-looking powder – usually white – that covers all or part of a plant.

Caryopsis: a dry seed-like fruit whose pericarp (the part of the fruit enclosing the seed) is fused to the seed coat of the single seed, and which does not open spontaneously on ripening.

Cespitose: growing in dense tufts or clumps. Describes bamboos whose rhizomes are "clumping" as opposed to "running", and which therefore do not tend to develop along the surface of the soil.

Chelate: a chemical compound whose molecules contain metal (iron) atoms.

Chlorosis: a lack of iron characterized in plants by an, often intense, yellowing of the leaves.

Cilium (pl. cilia): one of the marginal hairs bordering the auricle.

Clone: all the plants reproduced, vegetatively, from a single parent plant. In theory, all the plants from the same clone have the same genotype (genetic inheritance).

Culm: the main stem of the Gramineae (grasses). The stem of a bamboo is also referred to as a cane.

Culm sheath: the plant casing (similar to a leaf) that protects the young bamboo shoot during growth.

Genus (pl. genera): a subdivision of a family of plants with structural characteristics in common, usually containing one or more species.

Gregarious flowering: usually occurs when all the plants in a single clone (which has been repeatedly divided and distributed) flower at about the same time.

Internode: the part of the culm, branch, or rhizome between two nodes.

Leptomorphic: describes the long, thin rhizome typical of running bamboos. These rhizomes are usually thinner than the culms they produce and their internodes are long, slender and hollow.

Ligule: a strap-shaped membranous outgrowth occurring at the junction of the leaf blade and sheath in many grasses.

Monopodial: describes the growth habit of the rhizomes of running bamboos. The main rhizome continues to grow underground, with some buds producing side shoots (new rhizomes) and others producing aerial shoots (new culms).

Pachymorphic: describes the rhizomes of cespitose (clumping) bamboos. They are short and usually thicker than the culm produced by the terminal bud. These rhizomes have a circular cross-section that diminishes towards the tip. The internodes are short, thick (except the bud-bearing internodes, which are more elongated) and solid (that is, they have no central cavity). The nodes are not prominent (they are not raised or bulbous).

Rhizome: an underground stem that grows horizontally.

Running: describes a bamboo whose rhizomes have a markedly horizontal growth habit, and tend to develop along the surface of the soil.

Shoot: the stage in the development of the bud before it becomes a culm with branches and leaves.

Sulcus: or internodal groove. A channel-like depression running down the internode from the point at which the branch is attached to the culm.

Sympodial: describes the growth habit of the rhizomes of cespitose (clumping) bamboos. The rhizomes emerge from the lateral buds of other rhizomes, while the terminal buds produce new culms.

Turion: the tender, young shoot as it emerges from the ground without branches or leaves.

Index

Page numbers refer to text or captions,
except those in italics, which indicate illustrations

Bibliography

AUSTIN R., LEVY D., UEDA K., *Bamboo*, Nissha Printing Company, Tokyo, 1970.

CROUZET Yves, *Les Bambous*, Dargaud, 1981.

CROUZET Yves, JEURY Michel, *Des bambous dans tous les jardins*, Dargd, 1988.

DRANSFIELD S., WIDJAJA E., *Bamboos : Plant Resources of South-East Asia*, no. 7, Prosea Foundation, Bogor, 1995.

FARRELLY David, *The Book of Bamboo*, Sierra Club Books, San Francisco, 1984.

LAWSON A. H., *Bamboos*, Faber & Faber Ltd, 1968.

LIESE Walter, *Bamboos : Biology, Silvics, Properties, Utilization*, GTZ, Eschborn (Germany), 1985.

McCLURE F. A., *The Bamboos*, Smithsonian Institution Press, 1993.

OKAMURA Hata, TANAKA Yukio, *The Horticultural Bamboo Species in Japan*, Hata Okamura, Kobe, 1986.

OKAMURA H., TANAKA Y., KONISHI M., KASHIWAGI H., *Illustrated Horticultural Bamboo Species in Japan*, Haato, 1991.

RIVIÈRE Auguste and Charles, *Les Bambous*, Siège de la Société d'acclimatation, Paris, 1878.

STAPLETON Chris, *Bamboos of Bhutan*, Royal Botanical Gardens, Kew 1994.

STAPLETON Chris, *Bamboos of Nepal*, Royal Botanical Gardens, Kew, 1994.

Dr SUZUKI Sadao, *Index to Japanese Bambusaceae*, Gakken Co. Ltd, Tokyo, 1978.

Useful addresses

There are a number of amateur and/or professional "bamboo" societies and associations.

The European Bamboo Society (EBS), founded in 1987, has branches in Belgium, France, Germany, Italy, the Netherlands, Spain, Switzerland and the United Kingdom.

Addresses for these branches can be obtained from the EBS co-ordinator: Yolande Younge-Petersen, Dorpsweg 125, 1697KJ Schellinkhout, Netherlands.

The 1st international conference of the EBS was held in Puerto Rico, the 2nd in Prafrance (France), the 3rd in Minamata (Japan), the 4th in Bali (Indonesia), while the 5th is due to be held in Costa Rica in November 1998.

– American Bamboo Society (ABS), 1101, San Leon, Ct. Solana Beach, CA 92075.

– Australian Bamboo Network, PO Box 174, Fremantle, Wa 6160, Australia.

– Bamboo New Zealand, PO Box 11, Fordell, Wanganui, New Zealand.

– China Zhejiang Forestry Research Institute, Liuxia, Hangzhou, China.

– INBAR (International Network for Bamboo and Rattan), 17, Jor Bagh, New Delhi 110003, India.

– Japan Society of Bamboo Development and Protection, Kyoto Municipal Museum of Traditional Industry, Okazaki, Kyoto 606, Japan.

Contents

EVERGREEN is an imprint of Benedikt Taschen Verlag GmbH

© for this edition: 1998 Benedikt Taschen Verlag GmbH
Hohenzollernring 53, D–50672 Köln
© 1996 Editions du Chêne – Hachette Livre – Bambous
Under the direction of Paul Starosta
Editor: Philippe Pierrelée
Text: Yves Crouzet
Photographs: Paul Starosta
Cover: Angelika Taschen, Cologne
Translated by Wendy Allatson
In association with
First Edition Translations Ltd, Cambridge
Realization of the English edition by
First Edition Translations Ltd, Cambridge

Printed in Italy
ISBN 3-8228-7759-X